EMPATHY;

Of Growth Through Pain

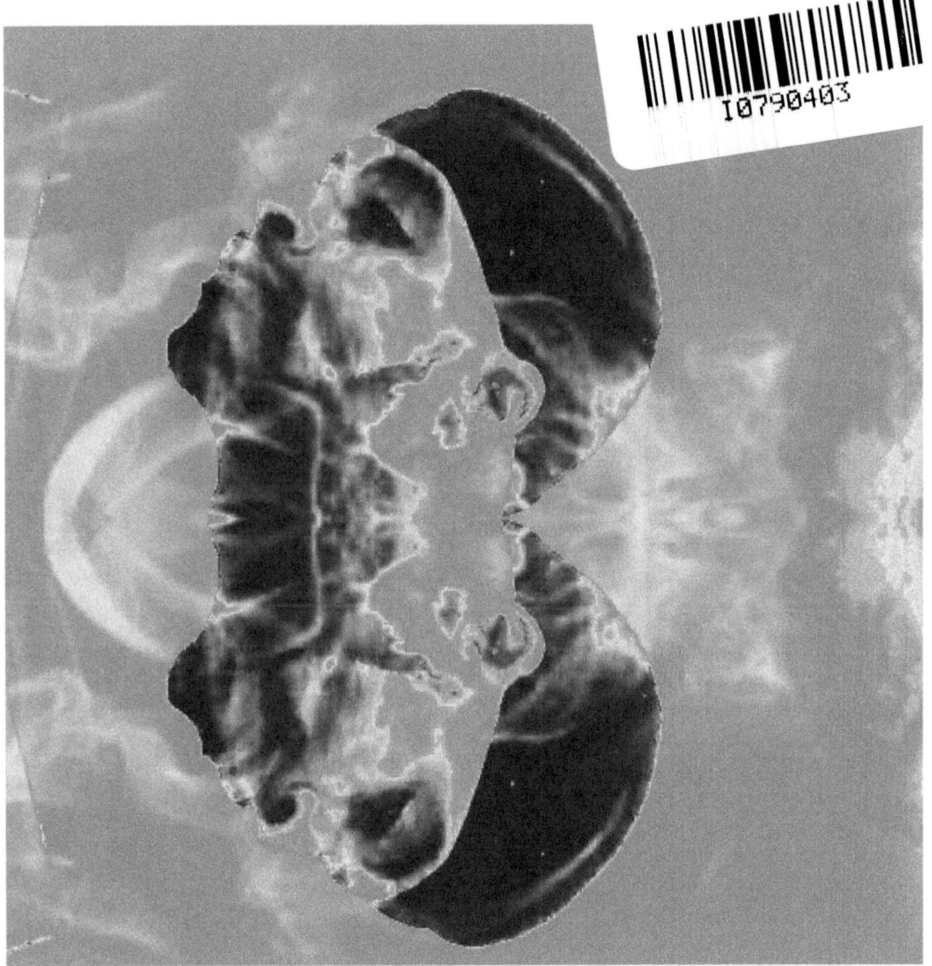

Written By: Antoine Dawkins

EMPATHY;

Of Growth Through Pain

Written By: Antoine Lendario Dawkins.   Copyright © 2023

Moon Walker, Publishing

"WHEN YOUR REPUTATION BECOMES YOUR GOD, AND YOU FIND YOUR SELF SERVING IT!"

-Antoine Lendario Dawkins-

THE EMPATHY OF GROWTH THROUGH PAIN!!!

I'M STILL SEEKING AN EXPLAINATION, IT BEEN PAIN THAT SEEMS TO HEAL US!

HEART BROKEN ITS BANDAGED/ SCAR'D VIEW ME ON CAMERAS/ TATTOOSIT AND VANDALS/ CAP'D RUMORED AND SCANDALED, MACK MULLAH GOD DAMNER/ IM BACK FLOWING MY CAMEL/ MY LAUGH MENACE MY grammar/ my smile wicked; and handsome... ... MY THOUGHTS ARE A BIT DARKER THEN MANSON'S

Table of Contents

Chapter 1
Need my Peace

Toine's girl Kia, had cooked dinner. During dinner, Toine received a text message from Peewee. Peewee had sent a text message to Toine, containing the addy of Broke. Broke was a nigha that Peewee had put on, in some round about way. Initially Toine and Peewee didn't know Broke from a can of paint, but had seen him around the city a number of times. Broke had caught a bid a while back. Broke's baby momma kept pulling up on Peewee, in the strip club. Ignoring Toine's advice Peewee fuc'd the bitch, anyway. Tossing her some crumbs and coins, was enough to put Broke on while he was in the can. After a while of fucking on her she got comfortable, and she started asking for shit for her self.

Girl name Tiffany, she a pretty bitch from the Westside of Atlanta. Peewee started pulling up more and more, so the pussy must had been phi. Peewee was paying bills, filling the fridge, even send Tiffany and her baby by the boy Broke shopping at some of the top end fashion stores and malls. It all went left one day after Peewee and Tiffany had fuc'd. While she was in the shower, the phone rang!
    Peewee presses answer on the phone control pad. Placing the phone to his ear, not saying a word just listening. The voice on the other end comes through, "Tiffany...!!!!... Tiffany...!!!... ... ... Hoe say something!" Peewee pulls the phone away from his ear and looks at the phone. "Shawty you got the wrong number, ain't no hoe of yours on this phone." "Bitch ass nigha, who the fuc is you and why is you answering my bitch phone." Peewee chuckles, "nigha check your temper and your hoes." Broke ignores Peewee's advice and continues his rant. "Oh, this that cap ass Westside nigha, Peewee. My partnaz that hustle on Campbellton, told me she had been fuc'n on you. Hope they told you, when I catch you imma kill ya." Peewee chuckles once again alight menacing laugh, as if the death threat he perceived as a tickle. As Peewee hears the shower water turn off he responds to Broke. "Ah Broke, you just bit the hand that been feeding you dawg. Well you barked at it. Howeva you want to play it, usually! Just with your statements, you got to go."

    As Peewee ends the call, Tiffany returns to the room from the shower. Wearing merely a smile and a towel, "Tiffany asked, " who was that?" Peewee removes the towel, as he playfully grabs Tiffany, on to the bed by the waist. "A damn bill collector, I'll take care of it, don't worry about it." Peewee lays back as Tiffany slides down and pulls his dick out though the slit of his boxers. As Tiffany sexually massages Peewee's dick, he turns her around so her ass & pussy are in his face.

Not breaking rhythm of the hand job, Tiffany kisses the head of the dick. Puckering her lips as she sucks merely the tip, while still working it with her hand. Tiffany then teases the dick by licking the head with the tip of her tongue. As Tiffany then takes the entire length of the dick into her mouth. Simultaneously Tiffany begins to moan and roll her hips, as Peewee sucks and fuccs her pussy with his tongue. Peewee suc'd her pussy and caught every drop.

    As Peewee rolled her over, she was exhausted from the tongue work. As peewee slid his hard shaft into her soft, and warm pussy, a light moan escaped his lips. Passionately Tiffany hit Peewee's shoulder, " nigha I know your soft ass ain't moan." Peewee kissed Tiffany on the chin, as he playfully whispered, "its my first time," while grinding his hips slowly into the pussy. As Peewee found his rhythm, in then out Tiffany's pussy tightened. Tiffany body jumped back, as if to escape the pleasure. Reaching for Tiffany's left leg Peewee hooked it around his back. As Tiffany wrapped both her arms, under Peewee's arms hooking his shoulders, in an attempt to pull him in deeper. Picking up pace, Peewee pumped in and out, up and down, and grinding. Rolling his hips in circling motions seemed to soften Tiffany's pussy, even more. As gyrating his body seemed to increase the warmth and moisture of Tiffany's vagina. Peewee tried to hold up under the pleasure. Tiffany rolling her body under him and thrusting her hips upwards, each time he made an attempt at an outward motion, overtook him. The motion of the ocean, intensified the simultaneous sexual eruption of both Tiffany and Peewee. They collapsed on top of each other. Sleeping with one eye up, after the death threat from Tiffany's baby dad, Broke. Peewee reached for his .40 cal from the nightstand making sure the safety was off and one bullet was in the chamber.

Chapter 2
Dinner with Kia and Toine

   While eating baked boneless chicken breast, French fries, macaroni, and butter toasted garlic bread, Toine was mac'n his sexy girl friend Kia, that sat across from him. Kia and Toine had been around each other since childhood. Their timing was off, in the earlier portions of their life. When Kia was in a relationship, Toine wasn't and vice versa. Finally after Toine had done the undoable to Kia's ex, her and Toine have been inseparable since. Toine seen Kia coming out of the Kroger grocery store on Cascade rd., with a black eye. Toine then, contacted one of his associates and got the whereabouts of the guy Kia was dating. Once Toine received the information he needed, he kindly paid Kia's ex a visit. Never mentioning that to Kia, Toine just popped up at Kia's door step that night. The next morning, Toine and Kia awoke in her bed together, her phone was ringing. It was the coroners office, they needed Kia to come identify the body. In Toine's head he is thinking, " maybe I should've dropped that body to the butcher, let him be the mystery meat of the week."

   As Toine bit into his chicken breast, eyeing Kia across the table caused him to sexually lick his lips. Kia flirtatiously responds, " you better finish that chicken on your plate, looking over here like you ready to start something." Toine smiles, "bae this chicken good, had me thinking about sucking on two breast and two thighs." Kia laughs and throws a French fries across the table at Toine. Toine's phone chimes, its a text message from Peewee. "Cuz I need the boy Broke gone, like yesterday. He get out tonight at 12:00 a.m.. This his addy. " Peewee attached two photos of the street sign and another of the mail box of Broke's momma's house. Toine responded back, " I'll wave bye to the boy Broke by 12:25, no lie."

   Toine finished his meal, then made his way to the bedroom with Kia. The two loved and cuz'd for thirty minutes. Explaining to her he had to go handle some business, sparked a lovers quarrel for another fifteen to twenty minutes. The lovers quarrel, more like, " fuck you nigha", followed by soft kisses, and "nigha your ass better come back home," and soft moans of "just stay with me another thirty minutes." Nearly having to detach his self from his love for her, merely to leave her home alone so he could go handle some business. Its the same for a simple run up the street, real love hard to part with. Even if its merely for a couple of hours.

Chapter3
Business is Calling

Toine got into his whip, by 11:50 p.m., he was parked outside of the greyhound station in downtown Atlanta. Toine watched as a greyhound bus pulled in. As the passengers unloaded the bus, Toine spotted Broke exiting the Greyhound bus, entering the Greyhound Station from the outside bus loading and unloading area. Broke was wearing the Georgia Department of Corrections, release uniform. A white full length button up shirt, a pair of dic dawgs and a pair of bobo shoes. Toine kept his composure, as Broke exited the Greyhound station, eating what looked to be a hotdog it was now 12:12 a.m.. Broke crossed the street to the corner store.

Toine gets out of his car and post up on the scarcely lit side of the corner store. Broke goes to the counter and purchase, "a box of Newport's, ... one hunnits!" As Broke makes his was out of the corner store, he packs the Newport's in the palm of his hand. Broke isn't paying any attention to Toine, as Broke crosses the path of Toine. Toine had an all black hoodie on pulled over his head. As Broke walked past Toine, as if Broke was headed to the nearby strip club. Toine's hands were actively attaching the silencer to the Ruger, in the pocket of his hoodie.

The two shots to Broke's head couldn't be heard, due to the silencer, the music of the nearby Magic City Strip Club, and the traffic of Atlanta's downtown night life. Catching Broke's body before it hit the ground, Toine propped the body against the stores front, bricks. Toine figured passer-byers would believe it to be a wino. Toine makes his way back to his all blue Audi. Taking a picture of the cars dashboard clock, Toine then sends that photo to Peewee, as an attachment. As Toine begins pulling off from the curb in front of the Greyhound station, he sticks his hand out the window waving bye to Broke. The clock in the Audi's dashboard rolls over to 12:25 a.m..

Toine made it back to his crib by 12:50. Smacking Kia on the ass, Toine says, "wake up, Kia! My food getting cold." Toine rolls Kia over as she spreads her legs, and Toine begins succ'n and fucc'n Kia's pussy with his tongue.

Wealth, a laid bacc relaxed guy. He carried himself with an air that emitted confidence of intellect. Still in touch with reality, Wealth was humble. Seated in the drivers seat of his Cadillac CTS, Wealth watched and observed the pedestrians enter and exit the Greyhound station. The time was now, 11:49p.m..

Wealth's reason for being in the parking lot of the Greyhound station, was the arrival of a private associate of his. Wealth had been parked at the Greyhound station, for nearly an hour. With humility comes patience. Evidence of honest wealth, in contrivance of a buckeen. As Wealth sat in the parking lot, an all blue Audi R8 pulls to the curb. Wealth noticed the Audi, and nonchalantly began to look off. Immediately snapping his attention back to the direction of the Audi. Wealth contemplated where had he seen that car prior to tonight, and who the occupant of the Audi could be. Through the dark tents of the Audi, at the distance he sat in his Cadillac, Wealth attempted to catch a site of the silhouette. After squinting his eyes for a couple of minutes, the tint didn't give. Wealth figured the occupant of the Audi was awaiting the arrival of a friend or family member, as he was. Deciding to sit and wait figuring the occupant of the Audi would get out the car to greet his guest once they arrived at the Greyhound Station.

Wealth dialed the number of his private associate, no answer. Leaving a voice message, "this is Wealth! I've been here at this Greyhound station in downtown Atlanta awaiting your arrival. I've been here nearly an hour and a half. Call me soon, I'm waiting on you. You should've taken Amtrak." Hanging up the phone, Wealth's head drops nearly to the stirring wheel. When a man is in pursuit of love, it dangerous. Its stepping outside of his typical comfort zone. Beyond the board room, stocks, investments, innovation and corporate banking, is an unexplored world to Wealth, of emotions.

Shaking off the daze of self grief and unexplored emotions, Wealth looks toward the direction of the blue Audi. Things seem normal, as a guy comes out of the Greyhound Station, in a white long sleeve shirt and some khaki pants eating a hotdog. He crosses the street to the corner store. As that person goes into the corner store, the occupant of the blue Audi R8, steps out from behind the tents. Wealth notices the driver of the Audi has his hand in the pocket of the hoodie pull over he is wearing. Wealth keen to situation notices that the driver of the Audi is in pursuit of the person who just entered the corner store.

Wealth looked at the hoodie wearing, Audi driver harder. Intrigued by his question of whom the person could be. Wealth begins by snapping photos on his IPhone. As Wealth looked at the three photos he'd just taken, he recognized the identity of the Audi driver. The paparazzi photo shoot turned into video recording once Wealth noticed it was Toine. With a spiteful, villainous smirk etched on his face, Wealth began recording Toine, as he posted on the dimly lit section of the store front. As the guy exited the corner store, he walked directly in front of Toine. Toine had his hoodie over his head, an his head down. As the guy passed Toine, Toine lifted the gun, and fired two shots. Catching the body as it dropped, Toine propped it against the corner store. Wealth continues recording, as Toine returns to his Audi and pulls off waving good bye to the deceased.

Wealth was a pillar of the community. Wealth was at least two decades older then Toine. Wealth is a tech giant, with vase connections in many fields. Wealth is a recognized high roller. Getting money legally and illegally, its just when you are honestly rich or wealthy in this case, its all gains. Not neglecting mention of Wealth being a recognizable name and face amongst the elites, of the secret society of which Wealth is an honored and valued member.

Since Toine was a mere child, Wealth watched over him. Wealth would appear at some of the more troubling times of Toine's life. Wealth always welcomed Toine. However humble Toine was, he refused to be belittled or pitied. Toine always questioned, what did Wealth want of, or from him? Wealth merely responded when asked,

I laugh, with you thinking I want something of or from you. I offer a response, that I ask you to consider. What I want for you?... ... ... I'm sure it is more then you want for yourself. You lack the life experience necessary to know what you want in this world. Possibilities are endless, yet with lack of exposure, you don't know those possibilities are even possible. I want you to be a better you. If you are not ready, in due season you will be. You come to me, and from that day forth, you shall be a better you." Wealth had never let up on his pursuit of Toine. Wealth had a passion,... ... a passion for bettering people. Yet what was Wealth's intentions with the freshly recorded footage. Wealth was now considering applying some pressure. Though Wealth's initial intentions were genuine, questions of has his desire for Toine corrupted his character.

Chapter 5
Who is Toine?

Toine from the DMV area, Norfolk, Virginia specifically a seven cities nigha. He caught a life sentence as a child, for a homi. Not a homie, but a homi as in homicide. Toine had a opportunity like not other. He was released on behalf of two of the biggest names in hip hop at that time. Tupac Shakur and Christopher Wallace also known as the Notorious B.I.G.. Toine was that young kid that Tupac would often talk to and talk about in his songs. I tell you, Toine was merely a kid at the time. Everyone knew that meant a bright future, of fame and fortune. What Tupac and B.I.G., expressed to Toine was with great power came great responsibility. Keeping his word to Tupac and B.I.G., Toine didn't sign a record deal and continued putting in the work that was necessary for the advancement of the people.

The stipulations of Toine being released from the life sentenced he was sentenced to as a child, was dependent upon his behavior growing up, the governing bodies would determine if Toine had to return to prison once he became of adult age. Toine was monitored closely throughout the years. He was indefinitely suspended and expelled from all school sports and recreational activities. That stipulation was later backed by the inner city reform bill of the nineties, that was also referred to as the gang banging baby bill. The bill stated that all kids that were from gang related areas or households were not permitted to play school sports. That was due to the level of inferiority that the youth of the black community impressed upon the opposition of other communities and races. The youth of the predominantly black areas were developing quicker and advancing in areas of character and maturity that adults of other communities and races hadn't reached. Toine as a youth, caused many a men to question their masculinity without even trying. Moving to Atlanta, Georgia in the mid nineties, Toine continued living his life. Ask Toine then he'd tell you the same thing he'd tell you now. He religious, its just his way of living, but as for a Muslim or Christian, "I ain't one of them!" He won't surrender he won't submit. His religion is how he grew up and he won't turn from it, he a get cha lick back, one fight all y'all fight, make some sacrifices to pay them bills. Where being a father, a parent, a dad, a brother, a uncle, a granddad, a baby daddy, a husband, a protector and provider for his family, are the values and principles of his way of living, his religion.

Due to the stipulation being dependent upon Toine's behavior growing up, after a number of incidents as a child and teenager, on Toine's 18th birthday he received a phone call. The courts determined that due to Toine's behavioral history as a child and teenager, although he excelled in academia, he would be required to turn himself in. Toine got the call, telling him to turn his self in. Toine hung up the phone and turned and joked with a friend that was standing next to him on the steps of his college dorm hall. " I just got off the phone, it was the feds. They just read me a monopoly community chest card, go to jail, go directly to jail do not pass go do not collect two hunnit."

At that time Toine knew he had to make something shake. He went to selling his music he had written, to numerous artist. That was something Toine didn't like doing, at all. Having other musicians release his music was something dreadful for Toine to watch. Toine wouldn't debate or argue whatever problem would arise, yet Toine still, took it for what it was worth, even if it was merely a mark to stay one with him self at later times, or to merely send a message to himself years to come, or years that seemed to already had passed. Truthfully Toine made a lot of dreams come true, propelling some careers to the top, to giving fans an opportunity to be apart of the music that they so much loved. Toine's demeanor deceived many, not in a negative sense. Toine's nonchalant mannerism had numerous individuals and parties believing he wouldn't, when he would.

Chapter 6
Fuc'n around

" Toine where are you going?" Kia asked.

"To your momma house! Why?" Toine responded.

   Kia was seated on the couch, with her pretty as pussy hanging out of her little ass cheer leading shorts, in a white tank top with no bra. She sat up after Toine made that statement, and she threw the television remote control at the back of Toine's head. If Toine hadn't fuc'd her for three hours straight, once he came in last night, then Kia's aim may had been accurate enough to hit him in the head with the remote from a distance. The television remote hit the back side of Toine's shoulder and landed in the floor, then broke as the batteries rolled about on the floor.

   "Your ass better stop playing with me. Now where the fuc you going?" Kia looks at Toine with one of those serious, stern, sexy ass facial expressions. "Girl as much as you called me DADDY, last night. I'm going home to your momma house. Before she find out that me and you been in this bitch playing house and decide to whip your ass." Kia got up from the couch, then pushed Toine in the back. Then swinging a punch at Toine. Toine turned around after the initial push, in time to catch the punch with his left hand that Kia threw with her right. Toine then reverse the stance, by placing Kia between him and the door. Kia looks Toine in the face and says,

"Negus let my hands go!" Showing no sign of cracking, Kia then swings her left hand. Hitting Toine on the right side of his head. Toine then catches her left hand. Now with both her hands in Toine's hands he pins her to the door. "Kia who the fuck, you think you handling like this." Kia shoots Toine a light knee to the crotch. Playfully! She then says, "you nigha, now what I say," in a soft sexual tone. Toine keeps Kia's hands pinned to the front door, then moves his body closer, pinning her body to the door with his body. Toine has on a pair of grey Nike sweat pants, a white V-neck T-shirt, a pair of white and grey Nike Hurriaches, and a gold chain and pendant.

   Toine aligns his dick with Kia's pussy. As Kia's resistance and snatching of her body only arouses her more sexually. Now her feminine growl and aggression is subdued to merely a sexual yearning moan. As Toine leans down and meets her lips with his. Kia's desire for Toine overtakes her, as her feet are no longer on the floor, as her legs are now wrapped around Toine's waist. Pinned to the door still, Kia reaches in Toine's sweat pants and pulls out Toine's dick. As Toine pulls Kia's cheer leading shorts aside, Kia inserts Toine's dick into her pussy, letting off a moan of satisfaction.

   Toine took her from the door, to the couch. Stopping at the kitchen on the way to the bedroom, not missing a stroke on the way. While on the kitchen table, Toine got aggravated by the cheer leading shorts Kia was wearing and tore them off. Once in the bedroom, Toine's phone began ringing. Toine reached for his IPhone, yet Kia immediately snatched it from Toine's palm. Kia tossed the phone on a pile of Toine's clothes near the closet, and got on top of him and rode harder. Toine tried to resist, its just when Kia want her way, she going to have it. It went on between Kia and Toine for another two hours. Not stopping until they both released simultaneously, Kia then immediately fell asleep.

   Toine laid in the bed, with Kia in his arms for another ten to fifteen minutes. Within that time, at the frontal lobe of Toine's mind was his relationship with Kia. What was so special to Toine in his relationship with Kia, was the sibling nature. It was a brother and sister, Toine's view of his and Kia's relationship. It was being able to relate that closely, the want and desire for each other, and the kinship. As a black male and black female, a brother and a sister. Easing out of the bed to the shower, was all in the childish nature of this still being a young love.

Toine pic'd up his phone on his way to the shower. Kia rolled over briefly and spoke, "don't shower nigha. Go home to my momma house smelling like pussy!" As Kia rolled over a smile expressed itself on her face. Toine lightly tossed his iPhone in her direction, landing on her ass cheek.

Once showered and dressed, Toine grabbed his iPhone off the bed from next to Kia. Gripping Kia's ass cheek, and kissing her on the lips. "Baby get your sleep, I got some business to handle." Kia reaches for Toine's hand as he turns to leave. Toine responds, "Kia I'll be home tonight." Kissing her once more then playfully snatching his arm from Kia's grip. Kia reached for the remote from off the night stand, throwing it at Toine. As Kia threw the remote at Toine, her body fell limp. The remote missed Toine as he walked out the door. Toine spoke back to her as he continued to exit the apartment, "that's the second remote your pretty ass done broke today."

Chapter 7
Why Me?

Toine left out the apartment and got into his blue Audi R8. Toine got into the car starting the engine, as he dialed Drop on his iPhone. Drop answered on the first ring. Drop spoke, "Toine where you at?" Toine responds "on the way, I got your text dawg." "Nigha I sent that text three hours ago." "Drop, I'm on the way nigha! I was fuc'n and fighting with Kia." CALL ENDED!

Drop one of Toine partners from grade school. Before Toine and Kia got to fighting and fuc'n, Toine had got a text from Drop. The text read, "Toine the nigha Black just got out, he rolling around town looking for you. Get here!" In Toine's mind, Black can't want smoke with him. If Black did want smoke with Toine, Black already knew where to find him. With Toine's reputation, doubt it was gun play versus Toine, Black was seeking. Toine still wasn't consumed by his own conceit, and has never under estimated any opp. People often asked Toine why be so humble? Toine had a simple response, "applying six pounds of pressure ain't hard. I did it a number of times. Its about the aim, and that ain't mine. Get this money and enjoy life too the fullest, and make my tomorrows more promising."

Before heading to Drops house, Toine text his baby momma Keke. "Shawty meet me out front in ten minutes, with my bag." Keke and Toine had been rocking since teenagers. They fuc'd once and she got pregnant. Toine must had bust her on accident, he hadn't even knew he fuc'd her, home was playa like that. Truthfully Keke was that playa herself, but that's what Keke and Toine told everyone, neither were open books to the world. Toine and Keke may get into it from time to time, but they still rock steady. Keke not Toine only baby momma, Toine probably got more baby mommas, then he got kids.

Toine was in the phone with Nika, when he pulled up into Keke driveway. Nika, that's Toine's son, Cam's mom. Toine says, "Nika hold up, here come Key." Keke opens the passenger side door and throws the duffle in the back seat. Keke speaks to Toine as she closes the door, then walks around to the driver's side window. "Toine when you going to stop playing house with ya Barbie, and bring your ass home." "As soon as your trick ass, stop humping on all them hoe ass nighas Key." Once Toine says that Nika laughs through the phone. Keke says, " what bitch you got listening and laughing nigha." Nika chunk back immediately, "I'm that bitch Key now watch your mouth." Keke recognizes Nika's voice instantly, and takes the phone from Toine's hand. "Nika that's yo ass, sis?" "Yeah Key, how you been?" "I'm good, girl! This nigha handling his business over there, how he suppose to ain't he?" Nika responds, "yeah bills paid, food in the fridge. He better handle his over there how he suppose to as well." Keke leans in more through the Audi window, and kisses Toine on the mouth. Then speaks, "that's what he expected to do. He handle it the same over her." Toine kisses Keke again, as he grips her ass. Toine responds, " Keke and Nika, I got some business to go handle, tell my kids to call me when the get outta school. Me, Makenzie and Cam suppose to go shopping." Keke and Nika said they aights and goodbyes, hanging up the phones as he put the Audi R8 in reverse.

Chapter 8
Pilot in the Alley

Headed to Drop's dope house, Toine backs the Audi R8, into an alley. Getting out the car, Toine reaches for the duffle from the back seat. Pulling the Draco out the duffle, checking it. Everything appeared clean and greased. Loading a hundred round stock, putting one bullet in the head. Then placing one of the two fifty round stocks that were in the duffle in his pocket.

Toine had began to lock the car doors, when he heard a single set of foot steps, coming his way. As soon as the footsteps came into site, Toine was immediately relaxed. "Yo Toine! What's up? What's the move?" Noticing the Draco at Toine's far side, DLoc eyes grew big. Toine spoke, " headed over to Drop's trap. He called me telling me Black just got out and he looking for me. Chit smell funky! I gotta find out what's, what. DLoc takes a step back as if to think and direct his thoughts and next statement carefully, cause what Toine just said was contradictive of what DLoc knew himself.

DLoc says, "Hold up! Drop said what cuz? Naw, naw, naw! I was at the hot wing spot, Station 1 wings last night. With my girl Candace before we went back to the crib, we was getting hot wings, drinks, and cigarettes. One of Drop's little runners, in the wing spot trying to kick flava to two of the girls that was at a table eating wings, and fries. The young boi flamboyant, show off, braggart type, doing alot of phat mouthing. He got that, he got this, and he about to buy a new Benz. Suppose one or both the girls know him and say, "nigha you broke," "yo momma about to buy a new Benz, not chu." The runner say something about he the capo, and Drop the Don. Then the girl say your name. The runner, tender dick ass keep popping and say something about Drop about to get you out the way, and that Drop wanted him to do the job."

Toine look at DLoc then says, "that's for real. Then why you just now telling me." "Nigha I had my girl Candace call Keke last night. She just called me and told me you was on the way here." Toine says, "aight... Do me a solid!?! Go walk over there buy a OZ of purp, and peep the scene. Have your camera phone on wit me on video call." "Cool only problem cuz, its $250 for a ounce of purp." Toine peeled off $500.00 from his knot and passed it to DLoc.

Toine sat on the hood of his all blue Audi R8 with his draco at his side and iPhone in his other hand. Watching as DLoc approached Drop's dope house. DLoc shows Toine the squad of five young dealers and shooters on the front porch. Toine listens as DLoc says, "the one standing on the top step, talking on the phone with the bright ass neo like lime green on, is shawty from the hotwing spot. Toine says, "I know shawty. I'm the one that got him put on. I tossed some extra dope and cash to Drop a couple years back and told Drop to put him on. That's Lil Keyze, I knew...----...---"

Toine was interrupted by shouts of one of the guys from the squad, that's on the front porch of the dope house. As DLoc was approaching the first step, one of the squad members spoke up. "No video calls, no phone calls, no smartphone, no iPhone, no ear buds, no air buds in the dope house. Antoine Dawkins got y'all nighas walking around like super spies, or go go gadget or some chit. Any more invention ideas of Antoine's and y'all nighas a be wearing moon boots walking on clouds. Hang that shit up, turn it off and give it to me. Imma give you ya chit cacc on your way out."

DLoc did as he was asked. Turned the power to the phone off. Took the airbuds out his ears, and passed them to the squad member. As Toine's phone showed call ended, he had already heard all the details of what the squad members had asked of DLoc. Luckily before the call ended completely, Toine got to see the faces of all the runners, trappers, shooters, and pushaz that were at the door steps of Drop's dope house.

The squad nigha talks to DLoc briefly. "DLoc I know this ain't your first time here, what you acting brand new for, nigha." "Chit nigha I ain't new round here, I was out chere when your as was washing cars at choir rehearsal, for the church." The young boi chuckle, as he stands on the bottom step, with black jeans, black Nikes, and a black T-shirt. Through the young boi's black T-shirt, DLoc could see the extended clip protruding, from some type of hand gun. The young boi responds, "that was before I started getting paper out here. Now I go by Slo-mo, but I'd stop through the church on Sunday still to shake my devils. Hopefully the crooked, perverse ass preacher ain't trying to trick our people out they lives. Talking about surrender y'all lives and be a servant." DLoc really surprised the young boi ain't talking about nothing. "Slo-mo, its good to hear something for real, make me feel like you maybe something for real."

Slo-mo humbly responds, "I ain't nothing," then begins giving DLoc directions through the dope house. "Walk in, the living room to your right, don't go in there! The steps to your left, lead to the basement. Don't go down there! That door should be closed. Walk through the kitchen, down the hall. Its five doors down the hall. Two doors on the left, two doors on the right. One door straight ahead at the end of the hallway. Walk directly to that door, don't open no other door. Don't peep in no doors, and don't worry about nothing, that ain't concerning you. You open the wrong door and you might not make it back out. Get your chit and get cacc out here! Don't make me come in and get you cuz, that's on set."

As DLoc reaches the top step of the front porch, Keyze says, "hold up nigha!" Stopping DLoc in his traccs. Keyze continues, "Slo-mo, nigha your ass trying to get the spot robbed. You gave the nigha a verbal tour map, through the spot. Nigha could walk through this bitch with his eyes closed. You ain't pat the nigha down even a little bit. Just asked for his phone. The nigha started talking to your broke ass about church, you gave him the right of passage." Keyze turns to two of the workers and says, "Press and Stocc, y'all shake buddy down, before he walk in This nigha Slo mo think he in Hollywood, passing out tour maps of the stars. Did you even get the money?" Press, Stocc, and Left Side laugh. Press and Stocc both pat down and run through DLoc pockets. Pulling DLoc's .45, blue steel, from his back, Stocc offered it to Keyze. Keyze looked at the hand gun, and then told Stocc, "eject the clip, and toss it to Slo-mo. Put the gun in the shoebox over there, with his phone and chit." Keyze turn to Slo-mo, "nigha just hold that clip, cuz I doubt he would had hesitated to let you hold it, in the worst way." Press patted DLoc down again, told Keyze, "he clean." Keyze looks at DLoc, up then down saying, "go head nigha! Don't get lost, or make any detours."

DLoc laughed with a slight smirk, as he loc'd eyes with Keyze, on the way in Drop's dope house. In DLoc's mind he is thinking, "these rookie ass nighas, give me a tour map with no tour guide. Once inside DLoc sees the door that leads to the basement on his left, he could hear voices coming from that direction. Thinking thats probably where Drop was at, DLoc's jaw clenched a bit tighter. To DLoc's right he saw the living room. To DLoc's surprise the living room was unoccupied. What stood out was the huge punch bowl, of marijuana, that was on the table. Surrounding the punch bowl, was a box of 100 count Swisher Sweet cigars, with a shoe box next to that, and some staccs of money. Immediately DLoc made the inevitable detour. Taking a sandwich bag from the shoe box, DLoc noticed the contents to be an ounce of cocaine. DLoc got three more ounces, tied the tops of each of those, then slid them into his boxers waist line. Grabbing a hand full of blunts, pocketing those. DLoc then got two empty sandwich bags and filled them with, the exotic marijuana from the punch bowl. "Sour Diesel!," DLoc said as he bagged the weed. Holding a bud to the ceiling light, to view the black leaves and the other noticeable details of the weed. DLoc then seals the sandwich bags, and slides them into his socks. DLoc's attention then turned to the staccs of money, that were on the table. DLoc thought against that immediately, they may over look the weed, would blame each other for the missing blunts, just swearing they he smoke dawg baby, but the would definitely notice the missing money.

Getting out of the living room, DLoc is headed through the kitchen. DLoc notices a big ass deep freezer in the kitchen. Also in the kitchen is four big ass guys at the table, two Jamaican and two Italian. Two of the guys are counting money, one of the Jamaicans is stacking coke, and one of the Italian guys is standing over them all as if he is calling shots. The one stacking coke says, "Touch, who the fuck is that. Get him out of here we're working!" Touch looks up, see DLoc and responds, "Oh DLoc! Where the fucc had chu been?!!" Touch and DLoc knew each other from back in the day. Touch knew DLoc would actually take ever thing in the spot that wasn't nailed down, that included lives. That's if he choose to, and could sell a hooker some pussy.

DLoc responds to Touch, "I been good, Touch. I'm married now, two kids. I'm out the game, by choice. Working a nine to five, I got the day off. Just slid through to buy a couple ounces of purp to blow." Touch says, well DLoc you look good. Do your thing, we got some work to do. You keep your money though, its on me. Tell them I said hook you up, with a pound of whatever you smoking." "Touch that's appreciated. Is your number still the same." "Infact it is DLoc. I still have your number as well."

As Touch leans in closer to DLoc he tells him at a soft whisper, "got some business to handle that may get messy. You might want to get up and out of here, quickly. This may be Drop's dope house, its just that me and my guys aren't in agreeance with a decision that Drop felt like he could make if you know what I mean." DLoc replied in a low tone as well, "in fact I do. Toine sent me! So where is Black?" Touch spoke, " Black wants no parts of Toine. Black is in the basement now, telling Drop how dumb his plan is." DLoc responds, "well hit me or Toine in thirty minutes. Let us know what's up, exactly. I'm about to get this purp and slide out."

On DLoc's way to the door at the end of the hall, the first door on the left was open. Inside was a mattress with guns covering the entire bed spread. Boxes and wood crates all around, covering the floor. From the first door on the right, could hear the sounds of an orgy coming from it. The erotic and enticing sounds of numerous moans and grunts, wines of pleasure. The second door on the left was a bathroom. The bathroom, from floor to ceiling including sink, toilet, and shower were covered in plastic. Apparently Drop had the room prepared for the disposal of Toine. DLoc chuckled, and retorted to himself as he fought the rush of aggression and emotion, "naw we not losing Toine." The second door on the right was closed. DLoc tried the knob but it was loc'd. The last door laid center at the end of the hallway, it was loc'd as well so DLoc knocked.

A female came to the door, naked from head to toe. She had a nice smile, haha that was the last thing DLoc noticed. She opened the door all the way, then stepped back asking, "what you want DLoc?" "I came for two ounces of purp, and apparently some pussy!" DLoc suggested as he stepped bacc to admire the body of the dope girl. Her name was Jasmine. DLoc had seen her around over the years, just was the first time he'd seen her like that.

   Jasmine was five foot four inches tall. Brown skin, beautiful Ethiopian from the westside of Atlanta. Her thick ass thighs, with a pretty pussy that looked like it deserved a kiss. Jasmine says, "well DLoc we could do that. Just that your girl Candace, may beat my ass and yours. Now what you buying nigha, and I don't sell pussy!" DLoc says, " I told chu I came for two ounces of purp, but Touch said get a pound and its on him." Jasmine says, "yeah nice try nigha!" As she got up off the bed and walks to the door, brushing her ass and titties into DLoc on her way to the door.

   Jasmine yells down the hall. "Touch! DLoc says this pound of purp on you! What's up?!" Touch shouts back, "yeah I got you. Let me finish working in here. He good for whatever though. If he wanted you too, then jump your ass in his lap." Jasmine turns back around to DLoc, coming to within mere inches of DLoc. As Jasmine's hand finds DLoc's dick, she begins to massage. As she says, "Touch says whatever you want." As Jasmine finishes that statement, DLoc removes Jasmine's hand and steps back. DLoc says, "let me get that pound of purp, hopefully we could fucc at another time." DLoc was thinking to hisself, "if his good stealing ass didn't have four ounces of coke in his draws, he'd be fuc'n on shawty right now." As Jasmine passes DLoc the pound of purp in a styrofoam food tray. Jasmine reached to hug DLoc, DLoc smooth gripped a whole ass cheek while hugging her, then made his exit. Jasmine shouted behind DLoc, "imma call you!" Then Jasmine turn to shout a Touch! " Touch give me my mutha fuc'n money fool.!!!"

   As DLoc was preparing to walk out the front door, the basement door began to open. DLoc stopped briefly so who ever was coming out of the basement, he could see them. The door opened, and the voices continued, "yo Drop, I comprehend what you saying about Toine having the city loc'd." Drop says, " Black you can't comprehend that. Cuz its more then Toine having the city on smash. Its like Toine got us living like we his little nighas and we ain't. I'm not having that. With Toine out the way, TODAY! We be on top, how we suppose to be." Black responds, "I hear that Drop, but why the fuck were you on the phone with him. Telling him I just got out and I was looking for him. Drop, Toine was the only nigha in elementary school that had open murder cases." Drop pushes Black into the hall, as they clear the basement steps. Drop says, "stop being so fuc'n scary dawg." As Drop finishes that statement Drop notices DLoc. "How long you been standing there?" DLoc responds, "just came to pick up some purp. I'm leaving now. Soon as you get out off my way!" Drop continued on stepping into the living room. DLoc looked Black in the eyes and said, "when did you get out dawg?" As Black bacc peddled into the living room not taking his eyes off of DLoc. Black said, "DLoc I just got out yesterday." Recognizing the nervousness in Black's voice, DLoc continued his exit. Retrieving his iPhone, airbuds, gun and clip from the Squad. Then regrouping with Toine, in the alley.

DLoc told Toine, word for word what he saw and heard. Especially the bathroom covered in plastic, as to stop blood splatter. Couldn't leave out the part about Drop and Black's conversation, he heard as he prepared to exit. DLoc said, "Toine, them nighas scared of you dawg. I mean for real, that's what its about. You scare them, and they want your spot." Toine responds, "fears merely a mental challenge, it ain't real, its like hallucinating. Merely being aware that them boiz envious, is reason enough not to take them boiz lightly. Cuz applying five pounds of pressure, ain't the challenge."

As Toine finishes that statement, a text message comes to his phone. Toine doesn't recognise the number, nor does he have the number saved in his phone. Toine opens the text message.
"Toine.... Black not looking for you.
Nor is he with Drop, on whatever
plan he got. None of us are. Drop
back against the wall."
-Jasmine-

Toine passes DLoc his phone to show him the message from Jasmine. As Toine passes DLoc the phone, Toine ask "what's up with girl?" DLoc reads the message then passes it back to Toine. "I don't know enough to tell you trust her, she got a pretty ass pussy though!" They both share a laugh as Toine gets his phone back from DLoc and places it in the center console. DLoc elaborates, "truthfully though, we got the whole trap. All of em in there with us, Drop surrounded. I'd never tell you we could trust them though." Toine and DLoc drive through the hood, the first stop is by DLoc's crib, so he could unload all the weed, coke, and blunts he'd boosted from Drop's dope house. At the age of 35, Toine has two and a half decades, plus a couple of years in the game. So he knows from time and experience not to be stressed or stucc on one issue.

Toine pulls up to the curb of his cousin's crib. Peewee in the front yard, on the weight bench. A few of Peewee's partners with him. They rotating the bench press, the spot, and the dumb bell. Toine and DLoc enter the front yard approaching the weight bench. The four guys with Peewee, acknowledge Toine and DLoc, with head nods, daps, and whats ups. Of course as if on que, Toine and DLoc match the energy and return the welcoming. When you in the hood, matching the energy is very important. Its the difference between the familiar and the newbies. It displays a level of comfort, the validated and those that are seeking validation, two opposite ends of the spectrum.

As Peewee notices Toine and DLoc, he begins racc'n the weight bar. "49... ... ... 50!" Peewee's spot man Slinga, says "nigha you was just on 24, now you talking about forty nine, fifty. Everyone gets a laugh. Peewee sits up from the bench, breathing heavily. As Peewee is still catching his breath, he nods his head in the direction of Toine and DLoc. Between breathes of air, Peewee speaks." Toine... What's up cousin?... ..." Toine looks at Peewee and responds, "that situation got handled last night!" Peewee says, "he had to go. No other choice. You funny too cuz, I got the picture of the dashboard clock you sent me!" "Yeah, kept it cordial, I was waving goodbye to fool."

Unlike Toine, Peewee had a itch for selling drugs. Toine sold more drugs, then most pharmacist, it just required too much dealing with others. Toine wasn't anti social, nor did he have PTSD. Toine liked living, loving, and enjoying life. Hell everyone else would probably had aquired a desire to enjoy life as much, if they'd been through the hardships that Toine experienced. That's the unkindled truth, the empathy of growth from pain. Toine referred to loyalty, as a question; and viewed loyalty as something of a test. "Either him or I, Chit sound like Shakespeare. In a game or games, where each is in merely for their own win, or ownself gain. Loyalty is all too often an Achilles, the strongest and the weakest. One thing for sure and two things for certain, the game isn't an honest social setting, nor a family fun zone."

Toine says, "Peewee that pussy Tiffany putting on you, must be some true love in it. Cuz I was eating dinner with Kia when you sent that text." Peewee rubs his left hand over his mouth, as he thinks of the taste, then the feel of being inside Tiffany. Peewee speaks, "I'm hoping I'm right about shawty, myself. The sword that kill once, a kill again" Toine looks Peewee in the eyes, "well cuz, if you and her started, as her sliding on her man. That doesn't amplify, she is presenting loyalty to you. I'm a leave it at that though, cuz." Toine let's that settle on Peewee's mind and conscience. The power of pussy, it give life and it take life. That's what Kanye must had meant, "NO WOMAN, SHOULD HAVE ALL THAT POWER!"

Toine continues his conversations, "other then that. Got some snakes in the grass." Peewee and his crew grow attentive, like "WHO? WHAT? WHEN? WHERE? and WHY NOT?" Toine breaks it down, "DROP!" ... ... "Apparently his snake ass in his feelings. Jealousy on some bitch chit tho, got me feeling like I'm bringing the bitch out a nigha. He hit my jacc, telling me Black just got out and was looking for me. I pull in the alley down the street from Drop's dope house. I was checking my Draco, making sure it was greased and clean, checking the clips. I was about to go to Drop's spot, in the blind and handle whatever issue. Luckily DLoc came patting down the alley. He say Keke tell him I was on my way there. He go inside like he shopping for dope. Say they got the bathroom covered in plastic. C say, he heard Black and Drop talking, Black don't want problems. Just that Drop want me out the way, feel like he'd have the top spot in the murda game."

Peewee look to his crew with a stern expression and jaws clenched. Peewee says, "Toine do we wait till tonight, or ride now?" Toine responds, "let's go!" As they all head inside, Peewee leads his crew as well as Toine and DLoc to the basement. The basement is a man cave slash artillery bunker. They all grab assault rifles, handguns, clips, and ammunition. Peewee begins handing out bullet proof vest. Peewee says, "Toine, I just got these in from your brother KD. He suppose to slide through later with some more hand grenades." "I hear that, he suppose to got me some new Techs." As Toine made that statement, Peewee pushed two crates containing Tech 9's in Toine's direction. "Oh so this where bruh, got em stashed at!"

Peewee and his crew divided up. Peewee and his right hand man Slinga, jumped into Slinga's Monte Carlo. While Stop, Tear, and Can't Deny rode in Peewee's Hummer. Stop a Miami nigha, slim, dark skin, with palm tree dreads. Tear, sell dope. Tear don't work a job, don't celebrate Christmas, Tear sell dope! Can't Deny, a young hitta, grew up in Atlanta, Adamsville, zone 4. Played ball, a real superstar. Had bills to pay, had to put the ball down and join a grown man game.He put in work around the board though.

Chapter 11
When its time, we never hide!

   DLoc and Toine lead the way, in the all blue Audi R8. As the three car convoy pulled to the curb in front of Drop's dope house, the squad of young boys out front, second think their initial thoughts ofreacing for their guns. Their actions were haulted once they noticed the sticcs hanging out the windows that were trained on nem. The squad of young boys, made the decision that was best for them, and ran! Clearing the small four inch fence of the front yard, with lil Keyze leading the pack. That was until DLoc tripped him up. Lil Keyze crambled to get back to his feet. DLoc looked at Keyze as he told him, "Keyze you going to do what to who cuz?" Looking up as Keyze began to back peddle as he studdard, "n... uh... I... eye... ah..." DLoc clipped Keyze's feet from under him again. Toine said, "Keyze get your young ass out of here; I know your daddy. I'm ne one who gave Drop money and dope to put you on." Keyze took off running. Slinga had snatched up Slo-mo, another of the young boiz from the front porch of Drop's dope house. DLoc turned to Slo-mo, "get your young ass out of here too. Y'all two catch us at Mosley Park this weekend. We may have some jobs for y'all, and get y'all asses back in school."

   As the squad took off in different directions, Toine, DLoc, Peewee, Slinga, Stop, Tear, and Can't Deny made heir way into Drop's dope house. Toine cleared the front entrance, then proceeded inside to lock the basement door. DLoc cleared the living room to his right. NO ONE! With hand gestures and allowing the others to read his lips, DLoc mouthed that at least five to six threats, were beyond that point.

   DLoc proceeded to lead the way into the kitchen. Immediately upon sight of DLoc, Touch and the other three guys with him gasped, retaining control quick enough to remain calm. DLoc says, "Touch you already know what this about. Where Drop at?" Touch stood there, hands held high with a pulsing motion, he turned to his guys. "You all remain calm." Touch then greets Toine, "Toine! I told Drop that fuc'n with chu is a bad idea. Do you want to do the honors." Can't Deny, Tear, and Stop walked through the conversation, as they start through he hall.

   Can't Deny looked in the first room on the left, no one. Just a bunch of guns, some still in wood crates, and metal boxes. Tear turned and opened the first door on the right. Tear saw a sight that was pleasure on the eyes o see. Three women sprawled about on a circular bed asleep, none wearing clothes. Tear turned and shook his head no, to let Can't Deny and zstop know Drop wasn't in that room. As Tear turned to get another peak of he sleeping beauties again, Stop proceeded to the second door on the left.

   Stop began to peak in that door, from a crotched position. The sight he caught a glimpse of, caused him to stand tall. Pushing the door open entirely, Stop said, "y'all nighas flinch, and I dead y'all asses." Tear and Can't Deny moved in at the sound of Stop's call. As Stop took two steps inside, Tear and Can't Deny walked in on the eft and right of him. Relieving the two gun men of their guns, Stop directed them into the hall, and down on heir knees. Toine comes down the hall, then enters the bathroom. Standing over Drop's gagged, tied, bloody, and naked body, Toine notices that Drop isn't dead yet, but soon enough he would be.

   Black comes out the back room at the end of the hall, buckling his pants. As a still naked Jasmine, peaked out while wiping the corners of her mouth. Black said, "Toine this my gift to you. Thank you for all you have done for the hood." Toine squats down next to Drop, and removes the gag from Drop's mouth. Toine spoke to Drop, "Drop, I been good to you. I feed you, I'm God father to your children. I paid for your mother's heart surgery. Why me?"

   Drop looks up to Toine, with what was once admiration was now a glow of envy, hate and jealousy in his eyes. Drop coughs up blood, then spit it out. "You got it all, the women, the cars, the money." As Drop spoke splatters of blood ejected from his mouth. Toine said, "Drop, I got what I deserve. What I worked for, that's what I put in work for. To get here!" As Toine's voice began to rise, he stopped and breathed regained composure then continued. "I ain't become a hoe, trying to sneak into a nigha pocket while he sleep. You stood next to me yet prayed in my downfall the entire time. With that said, get your rest cuz." Toine grabbed a towel from the bathroom counter. Using the towel, Toine covered Drop's breathing passages. Holding the towel over Drop's mouth and nose, until the body convulsed the final time.

Closing Drops eyes for good, Toine told Drop, "see no more, get your rest." Toine, Peewee, DLoc, Slinga, Stop, Tear, and Can't Deny made their way through the hallway into the kitchen, as they began to make the way to the exit. Touch spoke, "hey Toine!" Hearing Touch call his name, Toine turned to make eye contact with him. Touch continued, "what do you want Black, Jasmine, the guys, and me to do. All our calls and moves were coming from Drop. Every play was getting personally established by Drop. Drop was a lousy friend, but a heck of a playmaker. Its the dope game though, his loyalty was only to his customers. Even then that just meant he'd always supply their needs for dope."

Toine response to Touch, "Touch you and the guys do an inventory. Make count of all money, all guns, and all other product. I need that tonight, you all meet us at Zip's club. Jasmine, Black, and Touch is there any more plays that's setup by Drop already, we need to know about." Jasmine says, "yeah I got two that I know of. Got Florida boi driving up here, this weekend. That's twenty bricks at twelve a piece. The second one, is the one that only deals with Drop. Drop's brother! He grew up on Ol Nat, south side. He got his paper up, he a East side high rise nigha now."

DLoc says, "so now how many bricks Drop's brother want." Jasmine says, "Drop's brother, Forfeit picking up fifty. We meet them at an old warehouse off Washington rd.. The unusually about ten deep, in man power. Two SUVs, two cars, and a packaging truck. More like one of them box trucks." "Is he expecting any of y'all faces, o do he only deal with Drop. Drop had lowered his guard and gotten comfortable. Feeling like he the highest of the high, he decided to delegate a number of times and sent me and my guys. Toine as cool as you and your guys are, you'd be a straight give away." Toine ask, "what makes you say that?" "Toine everyone knows you kill shit, PERIOD. That's a definite trigger an alarm with Forfeit and his guys. Like my brother Drop couldn't make it but he sent a well known hitter!"

Toine says, 'well Touch you all meet us at the club tonight, then we can finalize the details. Package enough product for them two drops. Do the inventory, dice the boi Drop up. We finish this tonight. This ain't no master slave relationship, I've never before asked or delegated chit like that at all. When it came to handling business, I handled mine. Y'all know the reason already, wanted it done right, so I do it myself. Since y'all involved already, this business, job need to be done do it." As Toine finished that statement, he and the guys made their exit.

Toine dropped DLoc off at his crib, after parting ways with Peewee, Slinga, Stop, Tear, and Can't Deny. They all agreed to meet up at the club, later that night. Toine went to visit his mother. Toine scrolled through the contacts of his phone, through the computer in the dashboard of his Audi. Toine reaches the contact that is labeled, "My Ol' Lady," then presses dial. Turning onto his mother's street, the phone continues to ring. A soft sweet feminine voice answers, "Hello!" Toine pulls into the driveway of his mother's house. "Hey Ma!" She responds, "oh Antoine, its good to hear from you." "You to Ma, I'm out front." "Boy why is you calling me from in front of my house, come in." "On the way in ma. Just want you know I miss you." Toine ends the call, and begins to exit his Audi, as he starts his path into his mother's house.

Other then Toine's legal troubles of being sentenced to life in prison as a child, he had a number of incidents as a teenager. Toine still handled his business, and took care of his family. Toine would attend school, make good grades. When Toine got a chance to strike, he made it happen. Toine would pull jobs from time to time, and would pay jobs to employ his mother, yet don't get it mistaken Toine's mother made it happen.

Toine's mother separated from his father, when Antoine was merely seven years old. By then Toine, had already been sentenced to life in prison. Fortunately Tupac Shakur and Christopher Wallace, aided in having Antoine released. Toine's mother decided to move Toine from DMV area, to Georgia, along with his two brothers. While in Georgia his mother hooked up with a guy, Kenny. Toine didn't know if Ken and his mother, had just meet, had been known each or what. One thing Toine knew from the start, every man had his own motives. To Toine, Ken was just a nigha fuc'n on his mom, and liability and expense to him. Toine eventually went from paying businesses to employee his mom. To paying two businesses one to employ his mom, and one to employee her man. You know all that tricking Toine mom was doing, it won't long before she was pregnant by him.

Naturally we look at man, and immediately think he has motives other then what is revealed. Yet the woman of this world, not merely in modern day society, all the way back to the starting of record keeping of history The woman has been a thriving an dominant force. Many men may talk over aggressively, threaten, and some of us may act on our threats or threatening thoughts. Yet a woman, going to act purely on emotion, but she going to get at chu. When she get at chu, it may not be the worst way, but whatever way best for her?

Toine walks in and hugs his mom. Toine hugs his mother every time, with the tightest, toughest, most tender hug he could muster. As Toine hugs his mother, the kisses her neck and whispers, "let me be dadd?" Toine's mother playfully pushes him away, and hits him on the chest. "Boy stop! You always playing, and when is the last time you called your daddy boy?" "I called him a couple of days ago, ma!" As Toine's mother led him into the living room they took seats. "Well that's good, how is he." "He doing good, he told me he spoke to you." "Yeah we spoke briefly." "Hopefully y'all, you and my dad, do that more often, ma." "Yeah, we will try Antoine."

"Thank you ma, I can only ask! Where is your husband?" "Ken in the hospital Toine. He needed lung surgery. He had been diagnosed with lung cancer." "Dang ma that's wild. How'd it go?" "The lung surgery went OK, but they had to do another surgery. A blood vessel burst, so the doctors had to go back in. That went well also. Then doctor say he'll be in the hospital for at least two weeks." "Ummm... ... Tell him I said, for him to get well. All that smoking done caught up. That's why I be telling y'all workout and strengthen y'all bodies and minds. So health problems, mental or physical won't be an issue." Toine mother responds with the eye roll as she looks off, and says, "well I'll remind him that Toine?"

"Yeah aight ma. Rolling your eyes, like you trying to whatever me. Had chu talked to your other two sons, ma?" "Little Elford came over last night. He just hugged me, and we sat in the living room talking the entire time. He doing fine as well as his son Cinco. That boy getting big. He playing all type of sports, and he good

Toine!" "Really Ma!" "Yes he is! Also little Aaron doing fine he just got married again. Him and Ani-ta. He say her name and sound it out like that. They just as happy together. His daughter, Tarianna doing great in school. She also excelling at sports. I told her and Cinco what you said about strengthening they bodies and minds. ... ... Antoine I could go on and on about them, but when are you going to find time for them?"

As Toine began to respond to his mother's question, his phone vibrated. Interrupted by the buzz in his hand, Toine views the name displayed on the called I'd. "UNKNOWN". Toine nonchalantly hits ignore, then resumes his response. "Ma I spoke to little Elford and little Aaron some day during the week. Had them both on the video call at the same time."

As Toine finished that statement, his phone buzzed again. This time it was a text message, from a (770) area code. Toine looks up to his ma and ask, "Ma excuse me briefly?!" Toine opens the text and the message reads plan and simple;

"FORFEIT!"

Toine looks to his mother, and hugs her. "Ma I have to go. Business is calling." Umm hummmm business. Probably one of them country ass girls you been plying house with." Toine laughs and smiles as he makes his exit.

As Toine hops into his Audi, he hits dial of the (770) number from the text message. With Tue phone sync'd to the in car computer system, the phone is heard through the car's speakers. "Yeah who just sent me this text.!" s how Toine opens the conversation. "Nigha what the fuck the text say, "is the response from the other end. Toine is merely driving no set destination, just knows, to get the hell way, from his momma and his momma house.

Toine says, "so what the fuck you texting me fa? What the fuck Forfeit suppose to mean to me?" "I take it you never heard of me then. I came up on the south side, moving weight. I'm Drop, younger brother. For sure I heard of you though. Toine! A real urban legend. A hood legend. You even had a game, all about you like andy man. Go in the bathroom turn the lights out, and say your name in the mirror three times. Like Makaveili... Makaveili... Makaveili!

It been a while since someone called Toine on those specific details of his past. Toine says, "yeah. So what he reason for this call." Forfeit say, "truthfully I looked up to you. I never told a soul. Yet I just got the call my brother Drop got put to rest. Let me guess you don't know him either... ... ... Yeah aight. Wish it hadn't come to his, you was really an idol. I looked up to you. You know what's next." Forfeit ended the call.

As the call ended, Toine came to a red light on the corner of MLK Jr. Dr., and Fairburn Rd. In thought, Toine hinking is Forfeit the type to get straight at him or do he involve other individuals that the issue doesn't concern it all. When at we, you can't determine the oppositions next move. You can only manipulate it and be prepared o defend against it. As the light went from red, to yellow, Toine noticed an all black van approaching on his ight. As the light rolled over to green, Toine eased his foot off the brake. The sliding rear door on the van, slid open. As Toine caught the glimpse of the two individuals inside the van holding assault rifles trained at him. Toine floored the pedal. As the van attempted to floor the pedal in pursuit, one of the vans occupants fell onto he road.

Toino pulled his Audi into the Wayfield Grocery Store, parking lot. As the van turned into the plaza parking ot, it rammed another vehicle head on. Toine peeped the accident, as he pulled the Audi to a stop. After emoving his Draco from the back seat, Toine approached the van with caution. As the horn of the van blurred attracting attention, Toine knew he had to move fast. The noise and commotion of the accident would soon be a crime scene of multiple homicides.

As Toine approached the van, he sent three shots, through the wind shield into the head of the driver. As Toine made his way around to the side of the van, the assailant, opened the slide door. Falling to the asphalt of he Wayfield parking lot, Toine did the undoable putting him to eternal rest. One shot from the draco to the assailants head and one shot to this heart. Toine began to return to his Audi, moving through the plaza parking ot in a low crotch position. Toine hears the shouts, "watch out!" "One over there!" Remember Toine was born n Norfolk, VA and spent a lot of time in the Adamsville area of Atlanta. Toine turns in time to see the assailant hat fell out of the van at the traffic light, weaving through parked cars with an assault rifle in arm. Toine hears he police sirens, whirling closer. Toine shoots three shots in the direction of the opp. Merely stalling long enough for Toine to make it into his car, and leave the scene. As Toine seen it, staying a second longer he vould had fallen into the hands of the law. Instead get out of there. As for the last opp, twelve would apprehend him. Just that left the possibility of one threat that could return to retaliate on Toine, if the opp was released rom police custody or got away from the scene. Toine had to keep that in mind, one opp was still living and breathing, which meant the beef won't over.

Chapter 14
What A Celebration

Toine sat in the parking lot of his and Kia's apartment complex. As Toine sat there with his hand on, the trigger of his draco, he decided to see what was what. Calling Jasmine and Black to find out what they knew. Black said, "yeah Drop brother Forfeit play in the gun game. Should've told you that then. I ain't told him chit if that's what chu thinking." Jasmine, swore up and down she hadn't told nobody, nothing. Black and Jasmine both took it as they had a weak link inside. They both agreed to let Toine know the second they found out any thing.

Later that night at the club, Toine pulled into the VIP section of the parking lot in a 2023 X5 BMW. Toine was laid back, with Kia in the passenger seat. As Erykah Badu played through the speakers. Kia wore a strapless all Blanca one piece with blue accents, custom designer skirt. That fit every curve, and complimented every detail of her existence. In some 4" inch stilettos that brought her 5'6 inch frame to 5'10. Toine standing 6'2 inches tall, dressed in some custom designs. Blanca slacks, blue belt, with a white dress shirt,mwith twin blue rib cage gun holster. As well as some custom all white dress shoes, with blue bottoms. All custom designed and tailored specifically for Toine and Kia, by their personal designers at Loyalty Deserve Royalty Clothing (LDR Brand) and Only Us Clothing of the Only Us Brand.

As Toine steps out the car DLoc and Candace pull up in a all white Porsche 911 with the outside accented in blue, with the blue interior with white accents. DLoc and Candace step out of the Porsche, dressed to impress. Toine and Kia are leaned up against the BMW X5, Toine has Kia in his arms. DLoc and Candace watch on, then says, "we going in the club or cacc to the house. Kia say, "DLoc shuuutttt yoouuurrrr ass up!" Candace says, "Kia what's up girl." Candace and Kia step off and engage in conversation, as DLoc and Toine embrace each other.

Peewee pulls into the VIP section of the parking lot, with Tiffany in the passenger seat of his Benz. With a fleet of four other luxury cars, a Mercedes Benz truck, a Porsche truck, a Audi, and a Lambo. The drivers of those were Slinga, Stop, Tear, and Can't Deny. Each had a beautiful woman in the passenger seat. These were not mere females in the company of the guys, but women. A female is merely the feminine make up, yet a woman is the level of maturity.

As they all gathered, the women all knew each other, the guys all saluted each other. They coupled up again, each woman on the arm of her man. On the way into the VIP, shouts came from the crowd. "Yo Toine, Yo DLoc!!!! Toine!!!! Toine!!!! Yo Peewee!!! Slinga!!! Toine!!! Can't Deny!!! Tear!!!! Yo Stop! Y'all get us in?! If Toine and the guys were some rookies to the game, it would had probably been a group of young girls. Toine and the guys so much of seasoned vets, it was the Squad from the from porch of Drop's dope house. Toine and the FAM continue into the club, covering the door charges fro the squad on their way in. To in slides the bouncer two thousand and gives him instructions. "Get the young boiz and all they with. Tell them to enjoy themselves, and all to join us before we leave. Understood?" The bouncer responds, "its your world Chief!"

Once inside the VIP section, Toine orders bottles of Hennessey, Cîroc, Grey Goose, Paul Mason, E&J, Most, and Ace of Spade, for the FAM to enjoy. You know Toine don't drink, so Toine orders fruit juice for himself. The DJ began to announce that Toine and the FAM was in the club. It would've been just to show love, but Toine and the FAM not the boastful type at all times. Toine sent a messenger to the DJ booth. DJ announces, "drinks on the FAM all night for the whole club. Must have I'd though. We not contributing to minors." Then retorted hilarics at the squad members, "talk young nighas should bne playing sports somewhere!"

As the club roared on Jasmine, Black, Touch and his guys made their way into the club. Black, Jasmine, and Touch continued to join Toine and the FAM in the VIP section, as Touch's guys stood posted at the entrance to the section. Keyze of the squad, noticed the arrival of Touch, Black, and Jasmine. Bringing it to the attention of the other Squad members, Slo-mo, Press, Stocc, and Left Side. Left Side immediately pushed the female off his lap, that was grinding sexually. She fell to the floor, and was slick stepped on by the female that was booty shaking on Press; as Press pushed her aside. Stocc removed his gun from his waist and checked the stock. Slo-mo helped the female up from the ground, as he encouraged the crew tomslow down. Slo-mo spoke, "slow down. Everything good with all them. Stay on point though. The way y'all just reacted, its some issues coming. Just not at this exact moment." Keyze acknowledged the call Slo-mo just made and saluted him, as the squad resumed they party. Press said, "look at them partying, living it up, in the VIP section. That's where we suppose to be." Keyze say, "so what you saying? You think we should've hit that cap ass nigha Drop." Left Side made a statement in agreeance, "LEFTSIDE!" Stocc said, "truthfully y'all know I ain't nothing. So to call it straight up, Drop was flamboyant and phony as hell to me. So I know he was to y'all too." Keyze chuckle out of a menacing smile, before speaking. "So now we pushing a what if theory. So peep this! When they hit Drop, Toine and DLoc told us to catch up with them tonight. That is why we here. Toine ain't the bitc ass nigha, Drop was though. So we play it straight up. Before the night over we pull, as they asked. Ask for our own plate. We grind and get of up from there. From here on, we won't let no more opportunities like that get by us." The entire squad agree in unison, "LEFTSIDE!"

In the VIP section, all seems to be going smoothly. The women are enjoying their selves talking business and fashion of heir own worlds. The guys in the zone, as Slinga, Tear, and Stop are talking to Can't Deny about the new artist he preparing to sign. Toine, Peewee, DLoc, Black and Touch are talking business at a circular sectional of the VIP section. Touch ran the inventory numbers, of the money, guns and products to Toine and Peewee. Black and Touch then presented the numbers of the gun distributor and the heroine connect. Unappeased by the numbers of the heroine dealer, Peewee spoke. "I bring better prices, with less risk. Which means, more money for all of us, and we cut losses. The travel is insured, with prepurchased routes. "Touch and Black fully acceptive of that, nodded in agreement. Toine said, "well all good, all fine there. I got a order for guns, order of a hundred thousand dollars." Touch said, "Toine that a clear our stock. I mean geez." "Touch don't sweat it. That's what we I'm the business of, buying and selling. I got another distributor, along the East Coast. We got to meet him at the ship yard this weekend." Black looked at Touch before responding to Toine and Peewee. "I'm in! However far y'all want to take this. Its all profit to me."

Toine said, "Black, Touch, I know you two are in, yet check this! I had a incident earlier today. A text came through from Drop's brother Forfeit. I was at my momma house, so I leave immediately. I call the seven seven O, number back. Forfeit run down his end, then bang on me. Im at the corner of MLK and Fairbern, the light red? A black van pull up, the slide door open. They got they toys trained on me. So I smash the peddle and pull into the grocery sto, parking lot right there. Y'all know the one I'm tal bout..... I make it into the parking lot? One of em the goofy ass nighas fall out the van at the red light. Once the van turn in to the grocery sto parking lot, it crash into another car, head on. So I get out the Audi and finished the driver and passenger of the van. The one that fell out the van at the red light, I shot at him. I ain't finish him though, twelve had got him. I need y'all tonstay on point, I'll have this issue finished by Sunday. If you all hear of any noise from the boy Forfeit let me know."

As Black and Touch began to mid in agreement and Black began to speak, he was interrupted by some commotion within the club. The DJ made an announcement, "shout outs! We have trap super star FORFEIT and his crew in the soot tonight!" Toine better tip the DJ cuz Forfeit was moving through the club with motive and malice in his eyes. Noticing his element of surprise had been blown, Forfeit continued in the direction of the VIP section. Forfeit's crew of ten were moving through the club, following Forfeit's lead. Keyze, Slo-mo and the rest of the Squad, jumped up and immediately began putting in work. As they commenced to jumping two of Forfeit's goons.

Toine told the women to make an exit through the rear of the club. Kia got the keys to Toine's X5 BMW, as Slinga gave his girl the keys to the Benz truck. As the girls left through the emergency exit, the guys checked their guns. Toine made his exit of the VIP, onto the main dance floor of the nightclub. DLoc came out the VIP section, behind Toine. DLoc sped up past Toine. Knocking out one of Forfeit's guys with a quick three piece. Slinga, Tear, Stop, and Can't Deny wasted no time, engaging in hand to hand with each guy that approached.

As the brawl ensued, the DJ spoke, "can we all just get along." No bullets were shot, merely punches being thrown. That type of regard for human life, lets you know the caliber of gangsters you dealing with. Toine scanned the crowd, no sign of Forfeit. As the bouncers began to disengage the fighters, Toine still hadn't spotted Forfeit. The DJ came over the loud speaker, "well y'all black asses ain't shot up the place. Proud of y'all for that, but the police out front. So Forfeit, get all your homeboys off the ground, and Toine get all yours off of Forfeit's. Y'all get out of here, and take y'all ghetto assess home. DJ ... Go DJ ... A.k.a. DJ might take ya how!"

Toine gathered the guys before they began to exit through the rear emergency exit. A text message came through, from the seven seven oh number from earlier. It was a picture of Kia, with a all chrome glock in her mouth. With a message that read, "how much you love ya bitch?" Toine ran to the parking lot, his X5 BMW was still there. The doors were ajar with, Kia's phone and purse on the ground, and keys in the drivers seat. Tiffany's, Jasmine's, and Candace's phones were also sprawled about the asphalt surrounding the car, the back seat of the car, and the floor of the car.

Peewee, Black, and DLoc caught up with Toine. Toine hit the trunk pop button, retrieving his duffle bag from the trunk. Toine said, "let's go FAM. They got Kia, Candace, Tiffany, and Jasmine." DLoc's eyes grow big in shock as he questioningly states, "Cuz they got who?! LEFTSIDE!" DLoc slides into his Porsche 911, as Slinga slid in the passenger seat. Peewee, Stop, Tear, and Can't Deny are joined by the squad, Keyze, Slo-mo, Press, Stocc, and Left Side. Keyze look at Toine and say, "Big cuz its time to slide and we here. You know what we bout!!" All at once the squad chant, "LEFTSIDE!"

Touch and his guys are in two Range Rovers. Leading the convoy says through the speakerphome that's osting the conference call, "Touch pull up in front, we headed to the warehouse of Washington rd.. The spot)rop usually met Forfeit for drops." Doing as he was instructed, Touch mashed the peddle pushing his Range Rover to the front of the convoy.

Pulling up to the warehouse, Toine instructed everyone to cut their car lights off. As they drove into the arking lot of the warehouse, the convoy had yet to be spotted. In the parking lot were two all black vans, arked near the load and unload docks of the warehouse. One of the black vans was riddled with bullets, and anged up. That was the van of the hit team, that turned victim as the made an attempt on Toine's life the prior ay. Looking into the black van next to that one, Toine grabbed Kia's 4 inch stilettos. Toine placed Kia's tilettos in the back seat of the X5 through the rear windows. Grabbing his draco, he looks at the FAM and ays, "let's go, they inside. No loose shots. The only light that was on, was on the far side. So that's probably vhere they at. We get in, get the women and get out."

They make their way inside through the roll doors of the loading and unloading dock. Once in the make their vay to the only light that is in in the entire warehouse. Coming in view of the light at the end of the hallway, "oine receives a text message. Text message reads, "I was right right pussy ass nigha would come for their iitch." As Toine finishes reading that message, the lights go out. Shadows of males with guns could be seen noving, where the light was. Toine sends shots into the far end of the hallway, in the direction of the shadowed nen.

Toine, Peewee, DLoc and Keyze turn the lights on that are attached tot heir guns. Dropping low in a :rotched position, they jog towards the room where the shadowed men had came from. Like deers in leadlights, the opposition were in sight. DLoc and Toine lit up the three shadowed men, that appeared in the ght. Reaching the lighted room, Toine peers into the room. Forfeit speaks out, "so you kill my brother. You kill ny brother! Now you come to save your bitch from me killing her."

Hearing the loading of a bullet into the chamber, Toine pushes the door wide open and enters the room with iis gun trained on Forfeit. Toine and all I'm his company enter the room. Kia fights against the rope and the :hair she is tied too, as Forfeit has a loaded gun aimed at her temple. Toine says, "so Forfeit this the second ittempt in 24hours. What you want?" Forfeit smiles a villainous smirk as he responds, "so you know I won't :top till I kill you." Toine's hardened facial features don't crack. Toine immediately sends, a burst of bullets hrough Forfeit. Forfeit's body dropped to the ground. Noticing they were out gunned, the few guys that were)resent on Forfeits behalf, merely surrendered. One made a comment, "I told Forfeit it was a stupid idea." \nother said, "why would he try Toine, "as he tossed his gun at Toine's feet. DLoc, Black, Peewee, and Toine intied and embraced they women.

After returning to the club parking lot to get their cars, they went to waffle house. Toine and the FAM nearly wenty five to thirty plus deep. They actually filled the waffle house dining area, as well as the parking lot and he parking lot of the hotel next to it. The waffle house was located on Fulton Industrial blvd., so people who Jrove by pulled over to join the crowd. You know this the FAM, that a turn a traffic jam into a block party. It went rom merely the waffle house parking lot and hotel, to filling the parking lot of the hotel across the street, the vlcDonalds, and the gas station.

Toine held Kia closer then usual, as he ate his Steak and Potato's, and feed her. Kia was in more of a)acified state then ever before. Toine feed Kia a fork full of steam and potatoes, as she looked into Toine's eye, :hewing slowly. Kia then snapped out of the trance, punching Toine on the arm. "Don't ever let that happen to ne again." Her voice began to crack, a wine escaped her lips. "Toine I'm serious!" "Alright Kia let me get you out of here." Exiting the waffle house, Kia was more attached to Toine then ever before. It was an attachment of unity, of oneness, of completion. Getting into the X5 BMW, Toine and Kia made it home.

Toine laid up with Kia in the house most of the day. When Toine began to get up and get dressed, Kia jumped up and began getting dressed as well. Toine looked over to Kia, "where you going?" "Where ever you about to take me!" "Kia I got business to handle." "Toine beside ever great man, is a even greater woman." "So you Maya Angelou now huh?" "Naw! I'm still shook from your soft ass getting me kidnapped, last night." After hearing that statement, Toine removed the distance from between he and Kia. With his arms wrapped around Kia, Toine looked into her eyes as he spoke, "Kia I got a snake in the grass. I know that's no excuse, it won't happen again. My word." "Toine I know you going to handle the issue. That's not my question. Just when!? When does it stop? Are we in this forever? Are you coming home tonight? Cuz I know I am, and your thug ass better continue to reassure me that! Am I safe to, is it safe to go open my boutique today! Do I need five or six goons on security? I just want you, but let me know Toine." "Kia we getting to the bottom of this now. You with me all day, and tomorrow you can return to your boutique, regardless the cost. My word!"

Toine and Kia, met DLoc and Candace at a pool hall off I-20 west. Kia and Candace went into a conversation about last night events. DLoc and Toine decided to play a game of pool as they discussed business. As DLoc rac'd the pool balls, Toine broke. Breaking the racc and the ice of the conversation. "Yo DLoc, last night was tough. We gotta end this, as quick as it started. Kia ain't content. As long as she ain't content, this chit ain't over. So DLoc what's the word on the leak in the crew or is it just the streets talking. I mean first Drop plotting on me. Then his team flip on him, and knock him over on my behalf." Toine ligns another shot, aligning the que ball with the purple four ball, solids. Taking that shot, Toine continues speaking. "Then Forfeit text messages me, I never gave him my number. Next he has the drop on me as I'm at a red light on MLk and Fairburn. Then he pops up at the club. Instead of swapping it out with me inside the club, he leaves. After getting tipped off, who tipped him off is the question. Forfeit leaves the club and intercepts Kia, Candace, Tiffany, and Jasmine on their way out the club. The question is who?"

Toine steps aside as DLoc aligns a shot. "Toine I got my eyes and ears to the streets." "DLoc I don't need your eyes and ears to the streets, I need em open to what's around me." "Aight Toine I got that! Imma certainly let you know. Just remember Drop's crew flipped on him, on your behalf. Aiming at you was truly a bad idea from Drop, I do admit. Now the loyalty of Black, Jasmine, as well as Touch and his guys are forever to be questioned." Toine picks up , "Those are three I thought of immediately. Its the game, they not hoes, they soldiers, killers, drug dealers, thugs and chit like that. Loyalty ain't something they lac'n cuz, in this game, loyalty is to a person's self first. So due to their morals they stand on, which is a key aspect when it comes to the measure of how much of a gangster or man a person is, they made the decision that as gangsters the were required to make. So as for their loyalty, its not to be questioned, yet they are deservant of their recognition. Their loyalty is to be commended. Would we, if put in those positions, be gangster enough to make those decisions or would we just nod and agree. Now as for each of their dedication and commitment to me, naw that's not where they loyalty lies. They are each loyal to their selves. They not faulted for that, they are aware of why they in the game, and it ain't to merely add to my bankroll. Black came in the game riding the wave, getting paper and he show that. If Jasmine had leaked that information, she damn shoul should not had kidnapped her self. What's up with your guy Touch though? When they knocked over Drop, he spoke straight to you. As if he knew yo, or was with just you!"

As Toine's question caused DLoc to scratch send the cue ball into the corner pocket. Toine retrieves the cue ball and began to align a shot. DLoc says, "I actually met Touch while I was in the can. I had been seeing him around over the years, prior to catching my bid. In the can, Touch was running with some mobsters. When that went sour, he needed some A&A. You know a little aid and assistance. I took it there, he paid top dollar. Other then that, I did a number of jobs he aware of, years and years ago. So figure he owe me some favors from the can, and he may be a little impressed by my performance. I still kept him at a distance, even in the can. Its just something was off about him. Imma look into him some more, though.

    Toine and DLoc talked some more, touching basis on a fee other concerns. As Kia and Candace called Toine and DLoc away from the pool table. At a booth for four, Candace and Kia had drinks and food waiting for DLoc and Toine. As the two couples ate, Keyze and Slo-mo from the squad walked in. Not noticing Toine and DLoc in the booth, Keyze and Slo-mo walked by the booth talking. "How we approach this chit, cuz?" Slo-mo asked. Keyze responds, "that's what we do exactly. Handle it! Touch an informant. We handle it how DLoc and Toine would. Then let them know once its handles. We wanna be big dogs, we got to move how big dogs move."

    Over hearing the conversation as the two youths passed them, Toine and DLoc were all years. Kia hit Toine's shoulder, "you better not let them boys do that!" Candace looked at DLoc, with a facial expression that non verbally expressed the same thing Kia just said to Toine. DLoc spoke to Toine, "that's the confirmations right there." Toine reached for his cell phone and sent a series of text messages. One thing Toine knows, don't fight fire with fire. That would only fuel the fire, and could possibly consume you. Besides, water works better when fighting fire.

    Keyze and Slo-mo continued shooting their shots at the pod table. Preparing to leave Toine, Kia, DLoc, and Candace stood up from there booth. Keyze spotted them, "yo Toine... How long y'all been here? I didn't see y'all when we came in." Toine responded, "Keyze I seen you and was all ears to your conversation, big dawg" Keyze showing merely confidence and growth' says, "so what you want us to handle that." "Naw, if you got to ask, it must be a sensitive situation. It a handle itself, or something. Like, a self check. Pep this though Keyze, I like your intentions, you to Slo-mo. Y'all know what I'm into, y'all know y'all still got options though. Both of y'all good with me. I got something for y'all, stay tuned in." Keyze and Slo-mo dapped up Toine and DLoc. As they prepared to exit, DLoc stopped at the cashier. DLoc slid four hundreds to the cashier. "They with us!" Candace took the remainder of DLoc's knot of cash and passed it to the cashier. "Mam, we will replenish their tab once that amount is exhausted. One of us four." DLoc looked at Candace and said, "woman them kids ain't mine." Candace respond, "boy your ass ain't hurting for no two to three thousand dollars. Let's go!"

Chapter 17
Final Say So

Touch was in his apartment, over looking downtown Atlanta. As Touch phone began to buzz, signaling a text message. Touch shouted, "Tiffany you going to bring me the phone or what." Tiffany long legs, sexy Puerto Rican, ass phat and look softer then goose feather pillows, perky breast with the always erect nipples. She walks into the room naked, carrying Touch's phone. Touch says, "Tiffany since you been fucking Toine's cousin Peewee you been dummier then usual. What he fuck your brain out." Tiffany tosses Touch's phone at him as she retorts, "whatever ass hole!" Tiffany turns to walk off with an extra sexual walk, that came from merely the mention of Peewee's name.

Touch gets the phone its a text message from Toine. "Touch that order for a hundred thousand, in guns tonight. Right now I got one for ten bricks. I'm cross town, could you catch it. Black and Jasmine been at the spot. They can't move, waiting on Florida Boi to pick up them twenty." Touch responded, "yeah I got that ten here near me." Toine's response read, "The shoppa name Final Play. He going to give you the money, get the work and he out. He say the water fountain, outside the underground. Y'all trading footlocker bags, in a hour and a half." Touch respond, "say less."

Mean while at the dope house, Jasmine and Black are counting money and serving the local dope boys that stop by. Jasmine's, as well as Black's phones began ringing at the same time. Its a voice message from Toine. Jasmine opens hers and Black opens his, "Do this exactly! Out twenty bricks in two duffles , ten a piece. Get two Duffles, fill with cash. Go through the back door. Toss those four Duffles in the trunk of the Yukon in the backyard. Drive into the backyard, directly behind the dope house, and exit their driveway onto the street. Drive to meet Florida Boi at the Kroger parking lot off MLK Jr., Dr.. DO THAT LIKE RIGHT NOW!" Jasmine and Black got up and did as Toine asked immediately.

Chapter 18
Heaven's Gate Open To A Select Few

Peewee was at his auto body shop when he got the call from Tiffany. "Tiffany you owe me for this one!" " Peewee when we start keeping count! I got chu. You know I got chu. I also got my guys in place, around the underground? Just make sure he there." "He'll be there." "Alright Tiffany, dinner tonight at your place?" "Yeah, you better be there. What you all wanna do with Final Play?" "That's one of our guys, release him around the corner. Tell him I got a bag for em." "O.K. Papi! I'm so sick of Touch's rat ass. Forfeits boys told it all too, Papi. So tell Toine to be careful. His name is at the top of the charts. Tell him Detective Jackson says shell make it all go away." "Aight I got a customer pulling up. I got to go. Dinner tonight, your place."

As Peewee ends the phone call, he removes the blue mechanic rag from his back pocket and begins to wipe his hands. The rear door to the Roll Royce Phantom opens, as an all white Gucci loafer with a white gold buckle touches the asphalt. Peewee approaches the Rolls Royce as the occupant appears fully.

"How are you, my guy?" Peewee asked. "I'm great. I'm here looking for... ...," as the man pauses his speech he reads, the name tag of the mechanic uniform. "Awwwww yes Peewee." "Peewee responds, "yeah that's me. Who you?" "My name is Wealth. I've gotten the word, of the demise of one of my workers. Believe you knew him as Drop." "Wealth, as you see I'm a busy man. So I must ask how does the death of one of your workers concern me." "Peewee I hope you see my clothes, as well as my car, and presence as the reassurance that I am someone. I am wealth." Peewee smirks, as a light chuckle escapes his mouth. "Mr. Wealth, no disrespect, clothes, cars, posture, and hand gestures with grace as to guide your words as well as your conversation speaks volumes. Still you being someone, and the death of your worker involves me, how? Now if this Rolls Royce needs to be serviced, that I can do." "As I said Peewee, I am someone of importance. Though I asked a question, I shall give you the answer. I wanted Drop removed. Removed from the world. Drop has been a disloyal employee. I got the word that you as well as your cousin Toine, committed that deed. As I said I shall give you the answers. I Wealth, was not merely the financial investor to Drop. I was also the life line that kept him alive. I now employ you!"

Peewee looks at Wealth, with an all questioning eye. "Ah Wealth, I own this auto repair shop. I'm not considering you a joke, but you employing me. Employing me to do what exactly dawg?" Wealth returns to he rear seat of he Rolls, rolling down the window. As the luxury vehicle begins moving in reverse, "I employ you to continue, your works. I shall multiply your Wealth ten foods. Also tell your cousin Toine, maybe he should reconsider. I Welcome You!" The Rolls Royce then disappears into the world.

Slinga came out of the business office of the repair shop and stands next to Peewee. "Yo Peewee who was that in the Rolls Royce." Peewee standing solid as a bronze statue responds, "Drops former employer Wealth." Slinga says, "that was Wealth! Billionaire Wealth!" Peewee looks at the distance the Rolls drove in the direction of. "Say hell turn a stash of a hundred bricks into a thousand. A turn one lambo into a dealership, and a four bedroom into a sky scrapper. All of it sound good, but good enough to get me to tighten up on security. Get the word to the FAM to stay on point. The money sound good, just something ain't right about it." Slinga immediately went to texting and calling the FAM and crew, updating them of the situation that has arisen.

Peewee slid a text to Toine;
"Toine the fool Wealth just left.
He voluntarily employed me and
thoughtfully suggested you to
reconsider."

Within minutes Toine responded;
"He can go to. A Fools Wealth!"

Peewee:
"That's something we can agree
on. As for Touch, Tiffany got her
guys waiting on him at the Under
Ground in downtown Atlanta.
Get him there like rn. Oh and one
mo thing. The third passenger of
that van, Forfeit sent. He still
living and Detective Tiffany say he
telling it all. Your girl Detective
Jackson at the precinct got you
covered. Cuz if not then he goes in
for the death of Drop. Jackson say
they going to bill him.".

Toine:
"Sayless. The thing about Wealth...
He made a couple issues disappear
for me. I don't owe him nothing. One
thing I tell you, he a man of his word.
He said it, he meant it. I never told him
no, yet he never told me what exactly
came with it. I'll get to him, and we'll
figure this all out."

Chapter 19
A Man That Is So Deservant

As Tiffany hung up the phone, she walked into the living room, of the high rise over looking Atlanta. As she closed the sliding door to the balcony, she was startled by Touch's voice. "Who were you on the phone with, Tiffany?" Tiffany playing her role to the fullest, "that was Peewee. We having dinner tonight at my place. Why? Do you want to come?" Before Tiffany could finish that statement, Touch had dropped the duffle bag from his hands. Those hands were now squeezing Tiffany's throat with all his mite.

Tiffany's feet were nearly two and a half feet from the ground. Touch spoke with a venomous growl, as his hands cut off Tiffany's air supply. "Tiffany listen to me! Listen to me carefully. You were merely another poor, sideline street stalker, that I took in. I cleaned you up, I feed you, clothed you, and even gave you somewhere to lay your head." Tiffany's feet kic'd at the air and nails scratched at the arms of Touch. With every kick and every scratch Tiffany's body seemed to weaken, more. Touch continued, "hoe keep kicking and scratching yo ass die!... ... ... First it was broke, and you loved the bitch ass nigha. Poor bitch you even gave birth to the boiz child. Now I asked you to suck and fuck Peewee, to get every piece of information and where about of Toine. You can't even do that properly. Hoe you done fell in love with him too."

Finishing that statement, Touch releases Tiffany's throat from his grip. Once Tiffany's body falls from the height she was halstered too, she collapses to the ground. As Tiffany gasp for air, Touch spits on her. Its a striking splat of spit, that extends from her forehead, across her left eye, as it begins sliding down her nose onto her lips. Picking up the duffle containing the ten bricks, Touch begins to make his exit. As Touch exits the high rise he speak back, "how get me every dime Peewee has in his stash at his place. Every house, apartment, car, even the grocery store Toine shops at I want a list of. You got three days." Touch then exits the high rise. Tiffany's gasp for air, turned into laughs with teary sobs, as she knew that would be the last time she seen Touch.

Chapter 20
Final Play

Final Play responds to the text message from Toine. "I'm outsode the underground now at the Water Fountain." Toine text Touch, "Yo Touch, Final Play at the fountain right now, where you at?" Touch response is simple and to the point, "walking towards him now."

As Touch gets near Final Play, he sits his identical footlocker bag next to Final Play's. Standing side by side, Final Play tosses a quarter into the wishing well. With his eyes closed Final Play makes a wish... ... . Five seconds past, till Final Play reopens his eyes. Touch says, "Play I presume." "Yeah that's me, and hopefully in that bag that's ten whole at a thousand and eight gram each, thirty six each whole." "Oh Toine mentioned you were all about business. What did you wish for." Reaching for the footlocker bag Touch arrived with, Final Play prepared to make his exit. Verbally as Final Play began to back peddle he spoke, "I wished for freedom. Just we get what we pay for. Twenty-five cents is a small payment. For the cost of freedom for some, has been the lives of many. I been making payments, in installments." Tossing a wad of hundred dollar bills into the wishing fountain, Final Play turns and walks off.

Touch stands briefly as Final Play disappears out of site. Touch notices two agents coming from the direction Final Play just traveled. Getting a grip on the footlocker bag, Touch turned in the opposite direction of the two agents approaching him. Fondling his waist with his free hand, in search of his handgun. As Touch's hand finds his gun on his waist he pulls it . Firing two shots in the reverse direction at the approaching agents.

Touch turned the corner and ran into the parking garage to retrieve his car. Touch was grounded by a shot to his ass cheek. As Touch regained balance, limping and favoring his wounded side, he reached the inner portions of the parking garage. Once out of site of the agents, Touch was grounded again crawling and panting for air. Touch was kicked hard to the rib cage. Blind sided by that kick, Touch rolled over to see if he could get a visual of his attacker. That kick was followed by a precession of kicks and punches. Once the beating stopped, Touch's eyes were swollen shut and stained with blood.

Even if Keyze, Slo-mo, Stocc, Press, and Left Side hadn't worn ski masks, purple, blue, and black bandanas to cover their faces, Touch still would not had been able to identify them. As each stood over Touch with their guns trained on him, they shot. Five shots could be heard through the downtown Atlanta air. Two sets of foot steps came rushing at the squad, hearing "freeze," "who is that," from the voices that they recognised as police. With the shouts of, "LEFT SIDE!," all five of the young nighas took off through the rear exit of the parking garage. As the police sirens now filled the air, the squad were no longer in site nor arms reach of the law.

Once settled and to a safe location, the squad would send Toine the final photo of Touch. As Keyze, Slo-mo, Press, Stocc, and Left Side were now a hundred and twenty thousand dollars to the good, they prepared for an even split five ways. Twenty four thousand each, the squad was now the illest young hittas in the city. That one play, with what ever each had in dope money in their stashes, them young boiz were up.

Chapter 21
Debriefing

"Tiffany hold! I'm a call Toine on three way and you tell him that." Peewee hits the option button on his smartphone, that enables the multi caller feature. The phone rings two times til a female answers. "Hello!" Surprised by the unexpected sound of a female voice, Peewee looked at his phone screen to reassure he dialed the correct number. Peewee spoke, "Kia this you?" "Yeah Peewee, what other woman answering Toine phone?" "Kia you got to pay me for all that type information. Plus me and Toine family, I can't give him up." Kia laughs as she hears Tiffany laughing as well. Koa continues, "Tiffany how you doing girl?" Tiffany responded, "I'm good Kia, Peewee got me running around this morning. How you been after the club situation?" Koa released an exhale as she began to respond, "I'm alright, I been with Toine all day. Just shaken a little still." Peewee interrupts, "Kia y'all two emotional ass women need counseling or a psychiatrist. Right now pass Toine the phone we got some business to handle." Kia says, "here Toine, its Peewee." "Cuz what's up." "Toine everything ain't go as planned with Touch. Tiffany on the phone now. I wanted you to hear it from her yourself."

Tiffany begins, "Toine its not all bad. The agents didn't get Touch, nor did they get Final Play. Play got away. Touch got away from agents, bit got knocked over by a third party. Touch was found dead in the parking garage nearby, with six bullet holes in him. Only one of the six bullets were from an agent. The other five were from five different guns." Toine said, "Tiffany I appreciate your work and effort. I decided to improvise, and have a few of my guys there, to intercept. I knew you were tired of playing house with Touch. Plus I couldn't let that snake ass shit slide. Touch giving Forfeit the drop on me. I had to get my lick back. Chit like my religion." Tiffany says, "The footlocker bag missing so who going to pay the guys." Peewee speaks up, "Tiffany, Touch dead you free to do what you want. You and your guys got Touch's stashes, cars, apartments and house. Pay y'all fuc'n selves!" Tiffany acknowledged that remark, and hangs up. Toine and Peewee then make plans to gather later and end the call.

Toine pulled into the Kroger parking lot on Martin Luther King Jr. Dr.. It was a busy day in Atlanta, the entire parking lot was full from front to back. Every store in the plaza was packed with customers. Parking at the far end of the parking lot, Toine sat with Kia in his passenger seat as he set up to surveillance the exchange from Jasmine and Black to Florida Boi. Something seemed off as Toine watched Florida Boi's movements. Florida Boi seemed a bit fidgety and nervous. Toine sent a text to Jasmine and Black,
"Hold on don't get out the
car yet. Something slick
off."

Kia tapped Toine's shoulder, directing Toine's attention to the two unmarked cars and the white under cover standing in front of a Kroger, in a predominantly black area of Atlanta. This specific area of Atlanta has a minor amount of Hispanics and possibly very few whites, if any at all. So the white, clean cut male, hair a bit frenzy, and a five o'clock shadow of a shave is extremely noticeable.

Toine text Jasmine and Black,
"Dead... Deal Dead! Pull Out!
Pull off slowly. Normal Pace.
Text him saying y'all be right
back!"

Jasmine and Black started the Yukon, and pulled away slowly. Toine continued watching Florida Boi's movements, and surveillancing the parking lot. One suit and tie popped his head out of an unmarked car. Raising his arms to the air and pointing at the distancing Yukon, in a questioning manner to Florida Bio. Florida Boi pumps his hands in front of him two times signaling the narc to be patient. Toine had seen enough and put his car in reverse exiting the parking lot, unnoticed he believed.

Toine drove down the street to West Major Park, where Jasmine and Black awaited. Toine pulls in and parks next to the Yukon. Black is in the passenger seat. Black says, "Toine what was that all about?" Toine responds, "we took out Drop. We knocked off Forfeit and his guys. We still dealing out of Drops Dope House. Even had wealth pull up on Peewee, with some type of proposition. Touch choose to be a fucking cock roach, so he got excused. That dope house should be getting ran in right now. Apparently by Wealth's team. The way Wealth explained it to Peewee, Drop worked for him. Wealth consider us disposing of Drop, a favor to him. Wealth supposedly feel as if he financed Drop's dope house instead of me, or Wealth opened his eyes and realized he got finessed somewhere. Wealth doesn't seem to be offering a proposition he is stating it is best to align."

Black and Jasmine are intrigued by Toine's spill. As inclined as they are, their facial expressions encourage Toine to continue. "Where I stand is at a decisive point. Although I made it through my trials of numerous legal issues as a youth. I hadn't done it completely on my own. Every decision I made was calculated. Every murder was justifiable, and for a real reason. You know where I'm coming from, we law. To protect and serve your family, your hood is without question. Just in a number of situations I had some odds against me. PREJUDICE! Some shit as simple as black and white. That's where Wealth stepped in. Me and Wealth had a number of sit downs. We've ate together, on a number of occasions. He was big on encouraging my elevation. With me being lit, crossing paths with him and he enlightened as well has been real and humbling. The air of prestige Wealth emitted, had the individuals of simple minded prejudices regarding him as alpha male. No lie! I ain't on his dick and I tell you this in front of my girl Kia. I was in the courtroom, in handcuffs. The judge a dip chewing, can hunting fucca from no coloreds welcome land. I had the body without a doubt, the judge knows for fact. The dead man was an old perf, liked molesting underage girls. I caught wind of it. The judge knew it, but had all ntentions on saying no bail. This first appearance. Wealth walks into the courtroom, looks the judge in the face. The states, "Free him! Justifiable!" The bailiff took the handcuffs off me right away. I walked out through the front doors of the courthouse. I crossed paths with that judge at a Braves game and he regarded me in a completely different light."

Black says, "so what's next?" Toine responds, "I got Zip on the phone earlier. He not opening to the public tonight, so we going to meet up at the club. You and Jazz lay low until then."

Chapter 23
Expense of Comfort

Toine pulled into the parking lot of the W hotel. They valet approached the drivers side door, "Valet Sir?"
Toine exited the 2023 G Wagon, passing the keys to the young black valet. As Toine opened the passenger
side door, holding Kia's hand as he assisted her to the curb. Kia spoke, "Toine what are we doing here. I didn't
come dressed for this." "Kia you look good sweet heart. I brought you here to relax in comfort. Now relax!"

As they entered the W hotel, Kia's eyes marveled at the luxurious interior. This wasn't Kia's first time visiting
the W. As Toine and Kia walked to the service counter, Kia said, "Toine I was thinking of the first time we came
here. We spent that entire day together. That night we came here, you had reserved the room for a week." "Oh
yeah. You remember that!? I thought you'd forgotten." "No I hadn't forgotten that at all. You'd just beaten that
double murder case. The judge that had over sentenced you for those armed robberies, and that warden had
been getting questioned about their corrupt actions and unjust antics. Things had been going your way."

The service clerk spoke, "Welcome to the W Hotel." Toine responded, "Yeah I got a reservation." "in what
name sir?" "My name Toine,... ... Antoine Dawkins." The service clerk began typing on the keyboard,... ... ...
"yes I see your previous reservation. It shows, you usually reserve the same room each time prior, yet that
reservation has been changed. Its no longer that room Mr.Dawkins, it has been upgraded to a suite. Actually
the most luxurious of all the suites of this W. It was by you... ... Hold on... ... The computer shows... Oh yes.
The reservation is still to you, but was upgraded by Mr.Wealth. Oh my, any friend of Mr.Wealth is certainly a
friend of the W. Here is the key card to your suite with this note."
Toine passed the two key cards and the W hotel brochures and do not disturb sign to Kia, as he began
reading the hand written note.
"To Toine,
    Yes my young friend. I've watched
    you grow. You've certainly come a
    long way. I was sure you'd come
    here after the events of the past few
    days. Sure your cousin Peewee has
    told you of our recent encounter.
    Dinner tonight, and bring your lady,
    I'll bring mine.
                Wealth

Chapter 24
Dining With Wealth

As Toine and Kia exited the elevator, the continued playing and touching, each other sexually. This degree of companionship, between the two was all the time. As Toine and Kia entered the luxurious restaurant of the W hotel, Toine began sliding his hand up Kia's panty less skirt.

Kia spoke to the hostess of the restaurant, "yes were here to join the party of Wealth." The female hostess touched the screen of the computer before her. Three seconds later, the hostess spoke, "yes, right thisnway." As the hostess grabbed two menus, she escorted Kia and Toine to the table of Wealth.

Wealth was seated at a table for four. As Toine and Kia came into site of the table and Wealth, Wealth was sipping from q flute glass, of wine. Cuddled under Wealth's expansive wing span, sat a beautiful, glowing, black, dark skinned woman. As she sexually laughed at the obviously enticing, statement, Wealth whispered into her ear between sips from the flute glass, her curvaceous body was complimented by the sparkling white veneers of her smile. Her sparkling white smile seemed to dominate, the competition of shine, between her teeth and the diamond necklace she wore.

Wealth spoke, "Antoine, nice of you and Kia to join us." Extending his hand to Toine, Wealth continued. "This is Lady Billions. Lady Billions this is Toine and his life partner Kia." Lady Billions spoke with a strong accent of an African Queen, as she began to speak the ears that listened heard what sounded as a purring roar of a lioness. Stund by the strength, beauty, and intel of Lady Billions voice, Kia and Toine could not verbally express what they'd just heard from her. Whatever Lady Billions just said, it seemed as food to their souls. Lady Billions was explained more by Wealth. Wealth spoke, "Lady Billions isn't merely from Africa she still lives in Africa. Both of our schedules are busy and conflicting, yet we've been learning to make time for each other." Wealth poured the flute glasses that sat before Kia and Toine, half full of the expensive wine he was drinking. Toine took a sip, as the flavors of the fruits, and the sting of the spoils rushed his taste buds. Toine was sure it tasted expensive, and asked the name of it. Toine heard every word Lady Billions said, yet once again stund by the beauty and strength of her African accent and voice, Toine still didn't know the name of the wine, just that it sounded beautiful pronounced under the strong feminine African accent of Lady Billions.

As the party of Wealth dined and drank, they engaged in conversation more. Lady Billions actually invites Kia and Toine to return to Africa with her. Toine and Kia agree to, just not so soon. Kia and Lady Billions had scheduled an hair appointment at Kia's salon. Also Lady Billions had discussed connecting Kia to some of the leading fashion designers in Africa. Wealth says, "Well Lady Billions and Kia, I want you two to excuse Toine and I. We're headed to the balcony area we have some business to discuss."

The two males, make their way through the dining area of the luxurious restaurant onto the balcony. Wealth pulls out a cigar case, makes an offer to Toine. Kindly Toine declines, "No, and thank you! I don't smoke." Wealth lights the Cuban, takes a puff, then speaks through the smoke, sounding calm and intelligent as the air of prestige he emits. "All these years... ... All these years, I've watched you. I hadn't intentionally taking a liking to you. From the first time I'd seen you, you stood out. As you continued to grow, you stood out more and stood up. When I started cleaning up behind you, and pulling strings to kick your mess under the rugs, it was with foul intentions on my behalf. I had no motive of having you under my wing nor thumb. I say that because I'm sure it may appear that way. I was in a position to help you, and I did. You seemed to have all pure motives and intentions of your own. Of all the young guys, I've crossed paths with its your heart... ... your heart that set you apart from the rest. They had heart as well, can't say they were heartless cowards. Just the quality of heart, along with the mind you posses. Now I have you here,... ... Your here! Your here dining with Wealth. You don't owe me a favor, you do owe me a dollar. I did from the kindness of my heart. Yet you've turned down every offer, I offered. Why?"

Toine wasn't quick to respond. Taking in a deep breath, Toine turned to survey the city scape of Atlanta. A few breathes later Toine spoke, "truthfully Wealth. Your pulling strings, I never asked for. You doing favors in my favor, I never asked for. As you said every time you made an offer, I declined. Any time you did act on my behalf or in my favor, you hadn't ask me was it OK for you to intervene. As for me fighting against the bigots of the systematic society that fueled the courts, and you being in position to ensue justice in my favor, I appreciate that. Yet for your motives not to be to have me as your pawn, you sure bringing all this shit back up." Silence filled the air of the balcony momentarily. Toine looked Wealth up and down, not to size him but to put him in his place and hold him down. "Now Wealth, if your actions were genuine from past to present... ... then why the fuck we having this conversation again. You heard me mention the list of buckeen I got out your way. What about the dirty politicians that I deleted, that wanted you black balled. If we doing well in the positions we are in Wealth, why complicate this?... ... ... Oh and Wealth pulling up on my family... ...dawg... ..."

Toine turns his head from the gaze of the Atlanta skyline to looking in the eyes of Wealth. With a stern facial expression, and hardened facial features, the type obtained from serving time in the prison system, Toine spoke. "That's the reason I turned down your propositions, the money. You don't know your fucking boundaries. The money done got to your fucking head. I'd fail myself if I was to got like that. Not to be victimized by the Wealth. To avoid siding religiously with women I purchased, to avoid being surrounded with friends I bought. Wealth never again,... ... never again feel as if you an buy me nor the FAM. As for business, you got jobs that need to be done, I'll employ my guys to get em done. Between us, you and I, some lines are to never be crossed. Our business is a partnership, not a dictatorship and nigha don't forget that. Don't let your Wealth consume you or be the reason you get consumed... ... ... Now Wealth let's go in here and enjoy this dinner."

Briefly the air was stilled. Wealth's facial expressions, show'd he was near cracking. No show of hostility, Wealth thought that to be obvious signs of a buckeen. However there was the show of disappointment, and a snobbish air of being unpleased. Toine knowing Wealth felt as if everything of life, has a price tag. The downside to living by such a morally compromising philosophy, is that everything in that person's life could be afforded, emphasizing the said person himself.

As Toine turned to return to the table, Wealth grabbed Toine's arm. Wealth's body was stiffened by the rage that was building with in him, due to Toine's decline of Wealth's final proposal. Haltered from his reassured next step, Toine looked Wealth in the eyes. Wealth's eyes now glowed of an emblazoned red, as he vehemently spoke as calmly as he could mustard.

"As I'm sure Peewee told you, I propositioned him. As for you, I suggest you rethink your previous decision to decline." Wealth pulls out his IPad mini, and began to display a video for Toine to watch. "Now Toine I was at the Greyhound Station awaiting the arrival of a private friend, the other night. My... oh... my, how surprised I was by your super star performance. Here you are as you pull to the curb in your remote control car. You watch your prey eat a hotdog. Then you let him make his final purchase, and watch as he take his last puff of a cigerette. Then powww... .... Powwww... ..." Wealth's narration of the video footage was amplified with hand gestures, and menacing facial expressions and movements. The narration was merely Wealth's boast of annoyance.

Toine says, "so Weaslty, I had you pegged correct from the start. You really are a slime ball." Wealth smiles with an air of arrogance as he responds, "its business. Whatever it takes, for the win. As I said, initially I had zero intentions of putting you under my thumb, yet you make it so simple. You record beautifully by the way. So let's get back in here and enjoy this dinner, we will discuss details tomorrow." Toine says, "let's do that!" Jaws clenched and continue to tighten, and Toine's temples began to pulsate.

Chapter 25
Trojan Horse and Gifts

Toine sat in the parking lot of Brownlee apartments in the Adamsville area of Atlanta. As Toine sat in his drivers seat, Peewee pulled up beside him in an all black G Wagon. Toine began texting Keyze, "yo Keyze come outside." Peewee jumped out the G Wagon and slid into the passenger seat of Toine's Audi.

Peewee says, "Toine how did the sit down with Wealth go?" "Cuz it was no less then expected. Propositions were made its just I'm not in need, neither are you. So what he saying sound good, just working for him don't interest me. Now he talking like I have no other option then to work for him. He'd show'd me a video of me at the bus station and how I handled the boi Broke. We can get into that some more later. Just know for sure I'm ten steps a head of him.

Keyze was exiting his apartment, when he caught his first glimpse of the G Wagon. Slowing his step, stopping to admire the expensive luxury vehicle, Keyze peeps through the dark tents of the windshield. Noticing the dealer's tag on the G Wagon, he continues approaching the Audi. "Yo Toine what up?" Tossing Keyze the keys to the G Wagon, Toine responds. "Glad you like it, its yours. Its a hundred grand in the back, in Duffles. A gift from the FAM to y'all boiz, I like how y'all coming. Appreciate the work y'all putting in."

Keyze looks to Toine then Peewee. Keyze reaches his hand through the window, and daps up Toine and then Peewee. Humbly Keyze rspinds, "appreciate y'all, for real." Keyze walks over to the drivers door of the G Wagon. Pressing the door unlock button on the key pad, then the auto start. As Toine began to reverse out of the parking spot, Keyze rolled down the window of the G Wagon. Thinking the horn twice to get Toine's attention, Keyze spoke. "Ah Toine, who the fuck is Wealth? Is he one of your guys or what?" Toine smashed the brakes hard as the Audi jerked to a hard stop. Toine had been fed up with Wealth. Now that Wealth's cards were spread out on the table before Toine completely, it was no question to what came next for Toine. "I know him, why what's up?" "He lucky to be here today. I was sliding through the cut the other night, like through London Town houses, then through Kushmen Circle round that way. He in the cut, ... Trailing me! I pulled my phi so quick, spent back round through the trees and was behind him with that, iiiihh at his neck. I let him live, and glad I did. He had a couple of his guys waiting for him on both sides, the entrance and the other way in. We walked e rest of the way, he talking money though all I heard." "Em... ... He talked money. I know for fact he could pull strings. He been round me a while to long, he made those SME offers to me. I been pacing it though, had to learn not just who but whaim dealing with. He snake though what I came to learn. He a bit to giving not to be a gimme. Stay on po------- ----"

As Toine was speaking Cheat was walking out of his apartment. Toine noticed Cheat in his side mirror and slammed the car to park. Opening his drivers door as he jumped out, Toine said, "that's that hoe ass nigha Cheat. That bum as nigha broke into my spot while I was loc'd up." Peewee rolled out of the passenger seat of the Audi, as Keyze followed suit. Putting the G Wagon in park, Keyze stepped out his new whip. As soon as Keyze took three steps in direction of Toine. Toine had already threw a right hook to the left jaw of Cheat. That right hook was followed by a quick left hook with some cut in it, and an over hand right. The first pun broke cheats jaw, and knocked out some of his teeth. The second punch landed to Cheat's temple, leaving him knocked out standing up. The third punch the over hand right, woke Cheat up. Toine threw the fourth and final punch of the fight, putting Cheat on his ass. Looking down at Cheat, Toine spoke, "boy your bitch ass stole from me. Your bum ass stole from me dawg." Keyze pulled his scrap and pointed it at the head of Cheat. "Toine you want me to do him?" Peewee reached at Keyze's hand, directing Keyze to lower the gun. Peewee says, "Keyze, that's one of Toine's cousins!" Keyze's eyes bulged looking from the face of Toine to Cheat, then from Cheat to Toine. Seeing the resemblance Keyze put his gun back into his waistband. Toine took two knots of money out of his pockets, and then placed them in the pockets of his unconscious cousin. "Cousin, get it together, and fast."

As Toine, Peewee, and Keyze walked to return to their vehicles, Toine resparked the conversation of Wealth. Nonchalantly as if he hadn't just been in an physical altercation, Toine spoke. "Yo Keyze, truth about Wealth everything ain't what it seem with him. How you telling me he pulled up on you recently, Peewee saying the same chit." The thought struck Toine like a lightening bolt. Thinking to himself as he leaned against the rear of the Audi, Toine knowing Drop was trying to take him out for Wealth. Toine analyzing the situation from a what if perspective. What if he hadn't analyzed this situation a week earlier, where would he be? If Toine hadn't put the pieces of this puzzle together for him self, the ones he loved the most would be letting him down right now as his pallbearers. Right now Lady Billions was on her way to Kia's hair salon, to get her hair styles before leaving the states. Toine struck by the thoughts made a scramble to the driver seat of the Audi. "Peewee and Keyze come on, I... ... ...

As Toine was speaking two charcoal black Hummers pull into the Brownlee apartments parking lot. Rolling down e windows of the Hummers, as they block the Audi and G Wagon in. Out the windows of the Hummers came assault rifles wrapped in black trash bags, with grey duck tape. Blah... Blah... Blah.... A precession of bullets reigned. Guns trained on Toine, he hit the ground.

Would Toine make it? Will he live through this slip in the streets? Is Kia safe? Is Kia going to live through this? How could Toine under estimate the power of Wealth? Does Wealth have a moral compass? Does moral compass even exist in times of war, does moral compass exist in war at all? Depend on the caliber of a gangster you dealing with, but never forget evebody ain't gangsters. So some rules don't apply to everybody!

Chapter 26
Every Action There is An Reaction

Toine was knocked backwards on to the asphalt, from the impact of the bullets. It seemed as though the assault rifles from within the Hummer were aimed solely at Toine. That targeting allotted Keyze and Peewee the opportunity to return fire. Peewee slung the tech 9, it opened up rapidly. As Keyze sends shots at the Hummers, hitting one of the shooters immediately with a direct shot between his eyes. Peewee handled the Tech 9 with the grace of a professional. Peewee swung the tech 9 from left to right back right to left, in sweeping motions. As Peewee sent shots, the shots of the opposition began to seize. Keyze crouched down low after finishing is clip. After reloading, Keyze still in crouched position made his way to the far side of the Audi to take cover and check on Toine.

Toine held his left shoulder, with a leak of blood flowing from his neck. Toine had been hit once in the left shoulder, grazed once on the neck, and the third bullet to the right thigh. As Toine was covered in blood, he still sent shots in the direction of the two Hummers. Keyze said, "Toine come on! Let's get you out of here." Toine with his back now pressed against the Audi in an attempt to regain balance makes a statement. "Fuck that let me finish this clip." Toine returned to his feet, while leaned over the top of the Audi. With Keyze next to them Peewee, and Toine brought a reign of bullets to the Hummers.

Now the Hummers are under fire from both sides. As Cheat regains consciousness noticing Toine under fire, He unleashes a flurry bullets from his Mac 11. Instantly killing the drivers of both Hummers. Within seconds Toine, Peewee, Keyze and Cheat had overtaken the two Hummer convoy of shooters. Toine waved to Cheat, to "come on!" As Toine directs Cheat to get in the G Wagon with Keyze, Peewee, and Toine pull out in the Audi.

As Toine pulled out of the apartments parking lot, he dialed Kia in the Audi's speakerphone system. As Kia's cell phone began to ring, Toine spoke, "come on Kia, pick up, pick up... ... I'm in the way!" After two rings Kia's answering machine came on. "Hay you've reached Kia, I'm probably in my shop righnow with a client. If your calling to set an appointment leave a message or text. Then I'll call you back. If your calling to cancel just send a text or leave a message, but don't go down the street and let them fuck your year up." Beeepppp*

"Hey Kia answer the phone." Toine's message is interrupted, as he squints and wines as the three wounds from bullets began to burn and ache. Toine then continues leaving a message. "Let me know you kright. You get this message close the shop ASAP, go to ya momma house. Call me ASAP. NO WEALTH, NO LADY BILLIONS!" Toine hangs up and now dials the shop's phone number. Toine is now mashing the gas peddle as he weaves through traffic on I-20. Toine is driving so fast it appears as if the road and the other cars were moving backwards.

The shops pH gone is answered, "Hello?... ... Original Beauty! This is second Beautician Stack how can we help you." Toine was relieved to hear Kia's younger sister Stacy's voice. By the calm of Stacy's voice, Toine was sure no trouble had welcomed itself nor unfolded in the immediate presence of Kia. Toine spoke, "yo Stacy, where is Kia?" Stacy responded, "she is with a client right now. I'll tell her to call you back when she is finish." "That may be to late Stag. What time is Lady Billions scheduled for?" Stacy said, "hold on as I look through the appointment book... ... ... Within the next thirty minutes."

As Toine began to respond he began nodding off. Peeeee shook Toine's arm, "CUZ WAKE THE FUCK UP! HERE COME THE EXIT CUZ! WAKE UP! WAKE UP! WAKE UP!" As Toine began to decrease the Audi's speed as he prepared to stop at the off ramp of I-20. Peewee said, "Toine stop the car let's switch seats, and Stacy whoever Kia got in the chair either you two put they bitch out with half a perm or take the bitch with chall. Close the shop and get out of there right now. Do what the fuck I just said! We was headed there but Toine got shot three times and now he noddong out. Lost of BLOOD! Stacy do you hear me?" "Yeah Peewee, I hear you!" "Then why the fuck is we still on the phone? Now do what the fuck I just said! Tell Kia I'm taking Toine to Grady." CALL ENDED--------

                                Chapter 27
                               Original Beauty

   "Kia! Kia!... ... ... Kia!" Stacy chanted as she made her way through the Original Beauty Salon show room,
towards the private section. The private sector of Original Beauty is reserved for the social elite, the privileged
clientele of Kia's. Just having a dope boyu couldn't get a female in there, it was some NFL and NBA wives that
couldn't get a reserved spot in the private sections. As women all the clientele of Original Beauty are welcomed
as and entitled to their own special treatment of very important people, yet the private sector in the AJC reviews
was mentioned as a piece of Heaven.

   As Stacy barges into the private sector of Original Beauty Kia speaks. "What is it Stacy?" "Kia we have to go!
Toine been shot!" Kia was stand briefly, til Stacy grabbed her shoulder. "Kia come on! Peewee said he taking
Toine to Grady right now. We got to go before your next client arrives." Kia snaps back to, lifting the hair dryer
from over the customers head. Stacy nearly snatches the woman from the seat, as Kia attempts to explain the
arrival of the emerging situation to her client. Grabbing their purses and keys as Stacy and Kia push the client
out of the shop. Once outside the shop, Kia turns to lock the doors of Original Beauty.

   Kia's nerves are a deck at this point. Her hands are terribly shaking, and trimbling as she scratches the door
lock with her key, in an nervous and emotional attempt to lock the door. Adding to the pressure of Toine being
shot, Wealth is across the street, in the rear of a Phantom Ghost, watching the pain and grief he has brought to
Toine's nearest and dearest love. Wealth tosses a half finished Cuban cigar, out the rear window other luxury
vehicle. Smiling a mischievous and menacing smile, Wealth chuckles and rolls up the window. Lady Billions's
hands began messaging Wealth's manhood through the thin fabric of Wealth's tailored trousers. "Do you want
me to do the bitch, Wealth?" Lady Billions ask, as she begins seductively kissing on Wealth's ear, then neck.

   The question of the existence of a moral compass in the time of war is present again. The touch of Lady
Billions had caused whatever pain or sadistic thoughts of Wealth's to take a back seat to his yearning desire of
more pleasure from the touch of this woman. That's what it truly meant to have a man by the balls. Wealth was
so consumed by Lady Billions, he was entrenched into the enticing fantasy of sexual pleasure. Leaning in the
direction of a sexual eruption, completely dispelled the thoughts of an explosion of a firearm. Lady Billions
wasn't confused, of her identity or who she is with but was confusing to others. Lady Billions was and stand
firms that she is the strong woman in the [side] arm of righteousness. Sisters are going to be sisters, even in
times of war.

   As Lady Billions began performing orally for Wealth, she waved bye to Koa. Although Lady Billions couldn't
see Kia, Wealth couldn't either as his eyes rolled to the back of his head, engulfed in pleasure. A blinding
pleasure, and evidence that a moral compass isn't merely present in war, yet a strong defense and affective
weapon.
   Kia and Stacy get into Stacy's Impala and pulls out of the Original Beauty parking lot. As Stacy pulls her
Impala into traffic, Kia is dialing Toine's cell phone number. Kia hears what sounds as a gun shot, which
causes her to jump. With Kia's eyes glued to her IPhone, frustrated that she hasn't received an answer she
questions Stacy. "What did Toine say?" Stacy caught the flash of what seemed to be gun fire through her
review mirror, from the rear tints of the Phantom that was suspiciously parked across the street from Original
Beauty. Stacy shakes his head, "Kia we got to get out of here." Pressing the gas peddle, increasing the speed
of the impala as she makes that statement.

   Kia ask again this time with more of an insertively aggressive tone, "Stacy what did Toine say?" Stacy said,
"Kia, Toine called and asked what time was Lady Billions appointment. I told him I'm the next thirty minutes.
Then Peewee said Toine was noddong off, link fainting because he had been shot three times. The Peewee
said he taking Toine to Grady, and to get you to close the shop and leave the shop right away. Peewee said
NO LADY BILLIOMS, NO WEALTH, and for us to go to momma house." Kia said, "Stacy we ain't going to
momma house. We going to Grady." With that said Stack switched lanes, making the next turn in the direction

of Grady Hospital.

Chapter 28
Love Him To Death

   Lady Billions was sexually devouring Wealth, which seemed to be more the way of a cannibal people. Consciously timing Kia's escape, Lady Billions performed the act of oral sex on Wealth, aiming to suck the life out of him. As Wealth's eyes closed and head fell backwards against the head rest of the seat limp from pleasure, Lady Billions fingered her hand bag. Removing her concealed blue chrome glock, she removes the safety. As settle as possible Lady Billion begins to load one bullet into the firing chamber. Removing Wealth's cock from her mouth, causes Wealth to open his eyes.

   Wealth's eyes abruptly opened as Lady Billions seizes pleasuring him. Only to stare down the short barrel of the blue chrome glock. "La... La... La... Lay... Wai... Wait... ...," are the words Wealth studdard and mumbnled as his eyes fully opened. Lady Billions strong African accent roars to life again, "No Evil shall spill the blood of my brother and sister!" Finishing that statement, Lady Billions sent one shot through the brain of evil. As Wealth's blood coated the rear window of the Phantom, the driver rolled down the window. Not looking back the driver asked, "is everything alright Mr.Wealth?" The driver asked again. "Mr.Wealth is everything OK back there. Still no response. Lady Billions layed limply along side Wealth in the rear of the Phantom as if she had been killed as well. The driver cleared his throat then asked again, "Mr. Wealth... ... ..." Receiving no response the driver turned and looked through the divide window. Noticing Lady Billions sprawled about limply and Wealth's head blown open the driver gets out and opens the rear door. Lady Billions releases a kill shot.

   Lady Billions lady like as ever, steps out of the Phantom adjusting the wrinkles of her dress. Reaching back into the Phantom, only to retrieve her hand bag. Snatching her six inch stiletto heels off, Lady Billions begins walking. As Lady Billions begins her walk she dials a number. No Answer. Lady Billions tries again. Still no answer, Lady Billion decides to leave a message. "Job Complete!" Ending that call Lady Billions dials for an Uber.

Other Books By Antoine Dawkins

✔ Polish The Crown
✔ Space Slot Park/ The Park
✔ Coming Soon Polish The Crown II
✔ Why Me

Morally I should be an Influence/ Swear ya up and down/ Picasso or even big drew it/ I'm telling stories I seen PAC and even B.I.G. do it/ grade school enshrouding pains, the other kids knew it/ hey shawty, I was scar'd before the tattooist/ my momma tell em I'm smart as fuc, I merely act stupid/ its only five pounds of pressure, who wanna act stupid/ want the truth I'm slick blue and handle business, like a black Jewish/ circle small I lost the flaw, the residue of what the cash ruined/ sunny days... Dawg my past luneared/ violent past rumored/ it probably scare ya, when I laugh through ya...

Trust issues is rampant/ I love the game, but it been tampered/ I'm noid like where the cameras/ my calling or just a scammer/ ten toes before the sandals/ no gossip/ no propaganda/ momma ya baby showing his ass, we out of pampers/ heart broken its bandaged/ scar'd view me on camera/ tattooist and vandals/ capped/ rumored/ and scandel/ Mac, mullah, God Damner/ I'm back flowing, my camel, my laugh menace, my grammar/ my smile, wicked, and handsome... My thoughts are a bit darker then Manson's...
No Response in my answers....

Imma be that God some day
Remove all these scars some way
Tears may stop, but the skies gone rain
And the pains a subside; cold king

I treat em like they the mob that crossed Jesus baby, and ride on them boys like its easter baby

Ain't much changed, since last time y'all visited the ------- hum? /Angels encamp us and God is Guarding us/ Death to them devils that plotted harming us/ anti social, like them voices started alarming us/ waking up to the screams remember we all was up/ I been through and had notta, fuck they mean hard enough/ and took the trips to the parlors, like I won't scar'd enough/

I would like to thank personally every person that inspired me. Not merely the individuals that inspired me to write this book, but to those who inspired me to write the books before this one. As well as all those who reached out to me constantly inspiring me to continue writing music and books. Its been. Long journey thus far, I've got an interested story to. The portion of this book that is true, closely basing the main character off my story kind of sort of. My name is Antoine Lendario Dawkins. I was born on October 22nd of 1987. I was sentenced to life in prioson as a child. Fortunately I was released on behalf of Tupac Shakur and Christopher Wallace. Depend upon my behavior growing up the governing bodies would determine if I had to return to prison once I became of age. On my 18th birth, it was actually October of 2005 when I got the call telling me to turn myself in. They didnt care what they could get me for, all they knew they wanted me.I had began inking and marketing the initial ideas and designs of the smartphones and I phones alike. At the same time, writing music steering the careers of young artist. As well as exercising my creative marketing genius, as I shop the initial ideas of the Beats headphones to Dr.Dre. Everyone in the game wanted a Beat by Dre. Knew it a sell.... Haha□ "I TOLD CHALL!□"

SHOUT OUT TO ALL THE WOMEN THAT GOT A MAN THATS INCARCERATED AND YOU BEEN THERE FOR HIM. IM NOT SAYING YOU JUST DEPRESSED AND BLUE DAILY TRYING TO BE ON STAND BY, BUT THEIR FOR THE LITTLE BIG THINGS, OR EVEN THE BIG LITTLE THINGS. SUCH AS PHONE CALLS, LETTERS, FOOD, CLOTHES, EVEN AN OUTLET FOR ALL THE PENT UP THOUGHTS. NOT HAVING AN OUTLET FOR THE PINNED UP THOUGHTS CAN PRESENT INSANITY. YOU KNOW EVERY WOMAN DOESNT HAVE HEARTS LIKE THAT TO BE PRESENT THROUGH WHAT EVER.
TO MY KIDS, YALL COULD BE THE GREATEST, JUST STRIVE TO ACHIEVE THAT. TO MY GRANDKIDS, GREATNESS IF FORCED ITS OBTAINABLE THROUGH DEDICATION, COMMITANCE... TO MY CHILDRENS AND GRANDCHILDREN. NEVER SURRENDER, NEVER SUBMIT. THAT DOESNT MEAN BE REBELLIOUS, BUT ENCOURAGEMENT NOT TO FALL VICTIM TO THE DECEPTIVE SERPENTS OF THIS WORLD. NEVER SURRENDER YOUR LIFE, NOW YOUR FREE WILL. STAY STRONG
READ BOOK AND EXCERCISE
TRAIN AND STRENGTHEN YOUR BODY AND MIND

"They said the skies the limit. Then I directed their attention to the foot prints on the moon.! Moon Walker Innovations, innovating the way we line!"

Don Walker
Innovations